"Both in person and in his writing, Shak is like a very knowledgeable best friend: he lets you know that you are not alone; provides invaluable advice in easily relatable stories and illustrations; and always has your best interest at heart."

Autumn D. McCullogh

Attorney at Law

"This book is a must read for an underserved market. It is concise with easy to follow recipes to build a secure financial future for all women and their families."

Caryn Suffredini

Chartered Financial Analyst

"Shak writes with humor, informative and intriguing stories. They help me know what to do and what not to do. I strongly recommend this book to all women."

Maureen Dowd, of Florida

Also by Shak Hill

When The Doctor Says It's Cancer:
A Caring Financial Plan For Life

SECOND EDITION

A Woman's Guide to Financial Planning

*The Seven Essential Ingredients
For Your Best Financial Recipe*

SHAK HILL

Guiding Light Books, LLC
Burke, VA

SECOND EDITION
A Woman's Guide to Financial Planning
The Seven Essential Ingredients For Your Best Financial Recipe

Guiding Light Books, LLC books may be ordered through booksellers or by contacting:

Guiding Light Books, LLC
www.GuidingLightBooks.com
Shak@GuidingLightBooks.com

Because of the dynamic nature of the Internet, any Web addresses or links contained in this book may have changed since publication and may no longer be valid. The views expressed in this work are solely those of the author and do not necessarily reflect the views of the publisher, and the publisher hereby disclaims any responsibility for them.

ISBN: 978-0-9841334-3-7

Printed in the United States of America

Guiding Light Books, LLC rev. date: 1/1/2017

CONTACT SHAK
To book Shak for your events or
For more information and to order your signed copy, go to
www.GuidingLightBooks.com
Publisher@GuidingLightBooks.com

Your Financial Guiding Light™

This book is for Robin, my best friend, confidant, and mother of my children.

Contents

Acknowledgments

Not in a million years would I have thought that putting on paper the ideas and information that I have in my head would be so challenging! The tricky part was taking the sometime complicated financial topics and making them understandable. I hope you will agree this was accomplished with this second edition.

Special thanks to Robin for your patience, encouragement, and trust.

And I would like to acknowledge you for taking this important step toward your financial future. I truly wish you success and the ability to live your dreams.

Preface

Always bear in mind that your own resolution to success is more important than any other one thing.

Abraham Lincoln

The food in our home is always fresh, healthy, and delicious! My wife, Robin, cooks all our meals from scratch, and because of that I sure am one lucky guy. When a meal comes out of the oven, the kitchen aroma is that of care and love. "The best tasting meal starts with the best ingredients. Start with the basic recipe and add from there. Combine your ingredients in the correct order, and you will see the best results," Robin tells our children as she passes along the cooking traditions to them.

Choosing the right ingredients makes all the difference.

Consider the similarities of salt and sugar. They look the same. They both measure the same, weigh the same, and have the same white texture. If you substituted salt for sugar in a recipe, it doesn't matter that the salt was the purest, most expensive, highly recommended, quality ingredient. When misapplied, the best ingredients mixed in the wrong way will lead to a culinary nightmare.

Luckily, this is often not fatal nor is it the end of the world. You can overcome a botched meal by quickly cooking another one; you can jump in the car and go to the local restaurant; or you can call for some pizza or even Robin's favorite, Chinese.

This basic cooking message has relevance to those seeking financial advice and wisdom. You have to start with the best ingredients, create the foundation for sound financial planning, and add from there the unique ingredients that will help you attain your specific financial goals. You have to place them together in the right order and at the right time to get the best results.

There are times in life when the outcome resulting from wrong ingredients might be *financially* disastrous. You might not be able to overcome the error. There might not be an easy fix. Much can be lost with little hope to recover from your mistake. I offer my mother's story as an example.

My mother became single at forty-three. She was divorced after twenty-two years, and, in the settlement, she received a lump sum of money.

She lamented, "What am I going to do now? I have never had to make financial decisions on my own, *and* now I have this money and I have to make it last a lifetime!"

She had five sons aged twenty to twelve, with the youngest three still living at home. My oldest brother and I were already off at college. At age forty-three, Mom was on her own to make her own financial decisions. She was very smart but, like many women of her era, had never finished college and, until six years earlier, had dedicated her married life to raising her boys.

When my youngest brother went to first grade, Mom took her first job ever working as a real estate saleswoman, so she could set her own schedule around us boys. (She would later joke that it wasn't she who set her schedule but rather the clients.)

I asked her, "Well, what are you going to do now with your half of the settlement?"

"I am not going to make any financial decisions right now," she answered. "I'm just going to put all my money in the bank until I figure out what to do."

Years later, I realized that not making a decision **was** a decision. And it was not a good one.

Sadly, my mother passed away in 2000 at age fifty-eight. Her temporary "non-decision" to stash away her money into a bank account until she decided what to do appeared to be more permanent than originally intended. All her money was *still* in the bank and had not kept pace with inflation. Even her IRA was in a fixed account. There was

Unfortunately, she was on the path of becoming "an old lady on a fixed income."

no money earmarked for growth. Unfortunately, she was on the path of becoming "an old lady on a fixed income."

In many ways this book is dedicated to my mother who, due to lack of financial knowledge, didn't know how to make the best use of her money. This early personal experience with financial investment taught me the importance of sound comprehensive planning. Here is the story of how I furthered my education and am now able to assist others, like my mother, in making smarter financial decisions.

After graduating from the Air Force Academy, my next assignment was to flight school. I was becoming a pilot and thought I was cool. After all, the military trusted me with million-dollar jets so I had to be smart. Right?

One evening, my bride and I attended a financial seminar where we heard about a fancy investment. By using life insurance, we could invest money into the stock market and double our money in no time. The presenter showed us how the investments had performed and predicted even stronger returns in the future. (I don't think anybody predicts weaker returns.) At that pace, I would certainly be retired by fifty!

With reasonable risk over time, these investments should keep pace with inflation and even outpace it.

Attracted by it, we met with the speaker and bought what we thought would make us financially set for life. After all, I was *really* smart. Unfortunately, I hadn't remembered the old adage, if it sounds too good to be true, it probably is.

Life insurance is a wonderful financial ingredient and, when used correctly, can contribute nicely to a well-thought-out plan. But even the best ingredients used incorrectly can be harmful to the plan. The investment turned out not to be a suitable ingredient for my financial recipe. Fortunately, Robin and I managed to get all our money back.

Recognizing that I couldn't make many financial mistakes like that one, after flight school I studied finance and learned that there are wonderful alternatives between the two extremes of *too* risky and *too* conservative. From my risky extreme "get rich quick - sounds too good to be true" schemes to my mother's ultra-conservative extreme of "I'm just going to put all my money in the bank," there is a vast middle ground of proven and time-tested investments. With reasonable risk over time, these investments should keep pace with inflation and even outpace it. I'm not talking about the "dot.com" risk, but prudent, don't put all your eggs in one basket, diversified, and professionally managed risk that will allow even the most skeptical investor to do better than traditional bank deposits. Certainly, deposit items have their place, but not all of your money should be there.

After nine years as an Air Force pilot, I became a financial advisor.

Since joining the industry in 1997, my practice has gravitated toward the issues facing the woman investor. There are many circumstances in which a woman, who has relied on a husband, or someone else, receives a significant sum of money. Whether the money has come from divorce, widowhood, inheritance, or sale of assets, a woman can sometimes find herself unprepared to make significant financial decisions.

This book addresses women who now have to make independent financial decisions or who are seeking to educate themselves about proper financial decision making. You now have money and you need to find the best plan to ensure you have financial success and your goals are achieved.

Whether you believe the challenge of financial planning necessary, interesting or overwhelming, the information in the following pages will ease the stress and lift the veil of financial uncertainty. Together, we will outline a clear path for your financial recipe and decision making, ultimately arriving at your personal financial security.

What are the essential elements of financial planning? What are the ingredients that you will need for your financial plan? There is more to financial planning than just how much money you have. The *best* plan for you contains so much more.

In order to create your financial recipe, you also have to look at these seven essential ingredients to create the best plan. To help all better remember them, here is a fun acronym. You have to start with **A RECIPE**.

- *A* Desire to Leave a Legacy

- *R*ecognizing the need for a Plan
- *E*valuating your Wants, Needs, Goals, and Desires
- *C*ourage
- *I*nvestments
- *P*rofessional Management Team
- *E*state Documents Needed

This book is laid out in two parts. The first part addresses these seven essential ingredients and how to create your life's recipe. The second part focuses on a better understanding of the investment ingredients needed to implement your personal financial recipe. In the mix there are many fun stories to help you understand the sometimes complicated matters of finance. These stories may appear to be a little corny at times, but each one will help solidify the understanding needed to become financially successful.

Hold onto your apron. It is time to stir things up and create your recipe!

———

You now have money and you need to find the best financial plan to ensure you have financial success and your goals are achieved.

———

Part One

The Seven Essential Ingredients for Your Best Financial Recipe

Real-life stories, examples, and reflections will help you understand the sometimes tricky and always complicated topics of financial planning. You are about to discover the answers to all of your financial questions in a clear and fun way.

We are going to talk about

- The announcement you will never hear from the U.S. Postal Service.
- Your life expectancy and risk tolerance.
- The differences between a dream and a goal and reflections on the 1990s.

You are going to see

- A pyramid that you can invest in, learn what the vast middle is, and figure out why a super highway can help you stick to your financial plan.
- A clock that doesn't tell time and learn six ways to say, "I love you" as you create your legacy.

In addition to all of this, we will remember the Ringling Brothers, Barnum & Bailey Circus and why building your team will help you achieve your goals.

Are you ready for Part One? Are you ready to learn a lot and have some fun in the process? Let's get started!

A Desire to Leave a Legacy

The greatest legacy one can pass on to one's children and grandchildren is not money or other material things accumulated in one's life, but rather a legacy of character and faith.

Billy Graham

Who are you?

What are you made of? What do you believe? What are your accomplishments, great and small? When you leave, what are you going to leave behind? And to whom?

These are some tough questions to start a book about financial planning and creating a successful financial plan. But before you can move forward with the first essential ingredient, you need to know where you are, who you are, and what you want to leave behind. When you have a good understanding of this, you will start to know what your legacy will be.

What is your favorite family recipe? Think of when your mother, or perhaps it was your grandmother, made this for you. Did you help prepare the ingredients? Did you cut up the carrots, or measure the flour, or stir the pot until your hand was about to fall off ? Was this dish always served at a traditional meal? Perhaps Christmas with all the trimmings and decorations. Perhaps Thanksgiving with the turkey nice and browned!

I don't remember a favorite recipe, but I do remember every Christmas my grandmother would make all kinds of sweets, each from scratch. She would send each treat neatly tucked inside its own decorative Christmas tin container. She made all of the usual treats - sugar cookies with

*Part of your legacy is how
you transition your wealth
to your loved ones.*

Hershey kisses in the middle, homemade Reese's peanut butter patties, and, of course, chocolate chip cookies to die for! Every year my four brothers and I would sneak into the freezer (where Mom put them to stay fresh) and steal a piece from the tin containers. Every year we would wait for those containers to arrive. There must have been twenty tin containers, each with a different sweet inside.

My grandmother died from breast cancer when I was sixteen. It has been since 1981 when I last tasted one of her sweets, but the memory is fresh and the legacy she left is real.

While you were thinking of your favorite recipe, did it bring back special memories? Did it rekindle kind thoughts of a time well spent and hopefully still anticipated? These kind, heartwarming memories are the foundation of your legacy. For me, part of my grandmother's legacy will always be those sweets.

Part of your legacy is *how* you transition your wealth to your loved ones. You have the ability to take good care and set up the transition smoothly, or you have the ability to make it a costly and time-consuming mess. Do you know of someone who had a huge mess when someone else died? Were countless hours spent trying to square everything up, find out where all the accounts were? Where the safety deposit box key was kept? Where was the will? Did they even have one?

Hopefully the someone you know wasn't you. And hopefully you will be the someone others will remember who had their act together and everything in place. Remember, the last memory and statement you make to your loved ones is how smoothly and uncomplicated your estate transitions. I do not find it comforting at all when someone says, "Oh, I will be dead anyway, so I am just going to let them fight it out."

Generally that is exactly what they will do!

*Does your estate plan pass on wisdom and lessons
you would if you were still here?*

Colleen Barney and Victoria Collins

As you consider your legacy and how your assets are going to transition to loved ones, take time and reflect on the following questions:

- Who will distribute my assets?
- Who will inherit my assets?
- How are they going to be distributed?
- Do I give money outright or flow (schedule) to my heirs over time?
- If they are going to be scheduled, what are the "triggering" events?
- Who will be the guardian for my minor children?
- Who will be my guardian?
- Do I want the guardian to also have control of the money?
- Do I want my heir to have use of the assets but no ownership, thus limiting their liability?

In my personal plan, if my wife and I die while we have minor children in the house, we have designated one person to raise them, another person to manage the money, and a third person to distribute that money. We have intentionally created this process because we want the person who's caring for the children to not be burdened with money matters and vice versa. Each task is burdensome enough. Additionally, we are trying to make certain that the same person who is caring for them isn't also managing the money with the ability to distribute the money. We are trying to build in "checks and balances" for their care, if we are not the ones doing the caring.

> *The secret of contentment is the realization that life is a gift, not a right.*
>
> Author Unknown

Give Percentages Not Dollars

As you are writing your will, give consideration as to whether you give "hard" dollar amounts or percentages. It might sound nice to give $5,000 to each grandchild, but when you pass away ten to fifteen years (or more) from now, that gift might not have the same impact that you wanted. You may wish to give one percent, allowing for the potential growth over time. You could even combine the ideas such as, "I give each grandchild one percent of my estate, but not less than $5,000." Be careful not to have more than one hundred grandchildren!

If you are considering non-family beneficiaries, using percentages can be helpful. "I want ten percent to go to my church."

If you have any issue within your family, perhaps a second marriage, children from the first, Dad remarried after Mom died, anything that is out of the ordinary, read *Best Intentions, Ensuring Your Estate Plan Delivers Both Wealth and Wisdom* by Colleen Barney, Esq., and Victoria Collins, PhD, CFP®, Dearborn Trade Publishing, 2002. Especially read this if you have a large estate; this book is a must-read.

This wonderful book explains how the best intentions don't always happen, and how more often than you think, they flat out don't even come close. I encourage you to review their many stories just to see how vitally important it is to properly articulate your specific goals when it comes to transitioning your estate and leaving a legacy.

As they write in the book:

> "We know many clients and friends who focus only on probate avoidance or estate tax reduction when preparing their estate plan. We would like to challenge them and you to think about what your estate plan says to your family. Does your estate plan pass on wisdom and lessons you would if you were still here? How can you pass on your estate in a way that insures that you have provided more than just cash to your loved ones?"

They go on and ask three simple questions:

"Does your estate plan pass on wisdom and lessons you would if you were still here?"

1. If you die today, do you still have important lessons left to teach your loved ones?

2. If you could see what you left behind, what would cause you the greatest disappointment, the greatest pride, and the greatest sense of accomplishment?

3. What unintended message may be sent to your loved ones in your current plan or by lack of a plan?

WOW! These three questions are so powerful. They cut through a lot of the noise and chatter. They cut through the concerns of probate and taxes. Have you taken the time to write down your wishes? Have you articulated them to anyone? Perhaps you should.

Recently I met a new client, Debby, who I hope to work with for the rest of her life. Debby shared with me this story about her friend Beth:

> Beth is still working at age seventy. She is a hair stylist and barely makes ends meet. Beth told Debby one day that Beth's husband didn't believe in life insurance and now that he has died, Beth needs to work to make ends meet. Beth said, "I think he really didn't love me much because he put me in this situation." Debby told me, "At least my husband took care of me."

I was saddened when Debby told me this. What does your estate planning say about you? Remember, when we die, we pass more than money; we pass so much more, like family harmony, legacy, character, and lasting impressions, etc.

Set Up a System of Distribution

You may wish to give some consideration to labeling certain items in the home that you want to go to certain heirs. This way, there will be little dispute or bitterness from one to another. Of course, if you don't label everything, then that one item might be the item that is disputed. Additionally, if you use this idea, you will want to keep up with the labeling as you remove items and add new ones.

You may wish to ask the children and heirs if they have a "favorite" item. This may eliminate concerns that you have if one of them doesn't mention the items that the others indicate. If there is an overlap, then you can set up a resolution before there are any hurt feelings.

Unfortunately, I have seen some take the position: "Well, I'm going to be gone so they can settle it by themselves." Unfortunately, this attitude just might be passing along a lesson that you don't want it to. You might just be setting your heirs up for frustration, anger, and resentment.

You also may wish to write a letter of explanation as to your choices. Mention in that letter that more than one of you wanted this item. The letter might go like, "Family harmony is more important than any one item, therefore I'm going to decide so you won't be frustrated with the process." You might just be surprised that this course of action may be well received.

Of course, you could order everything sold at best value and the money divided.

> Dora knew that there was considerable friction among all of the children for one reason or another. She didn't want this to continue after her passing. I asked her if after she dies will anyone move in and occupy the home. She said no. She asked me what I thought if she just had someone sell everything and have the proceeds divided equally, "After all, they can't complain with cash because it will be even down to the penny." And this is what she did. She named the bank the executor and had everything sold and evenly divided. Interestingly, the kids were surprised by this at first, but then realized that it was the best decision that she could have ever made. Not only did Dora pass money, she also passed family harmony.

Don't Put Off Creating Your Documents

I hear time and again all the excuses for not getting important estate planning documents in order. You can think of many, perhaps you have either said them yourself or you have heard them. There is almost nothing that I can think of that should prevent you from moving forward with creating your estate documents, especially if you have important information about where you *don't* want your money to go, or if you have minor children.

Let me share with you a true story that occurred not too long ago.

I did not know Martha, but her family tells me she was lovely. Her death was welcomed after a long life and short illness. Martha had one daughter and one son. The son had fallen on hard times and was in trouble with an IRS judgment against him. To avoid her money going to the IRS, Martha willed it all to her daughter, who promised to share with her brother "under the table." I did not know Teresa (the daughter). She died instantly from a motor vehicle accident three weeks after Martha was buried. I met Stephanie, Martha's granddaughter and Teresa's daughter. She was Teresa's only child and inherited everything from Martha and from Teresa. Stephanie was twenty-two and in a relationship with a much older man (fifty-three). She relied on his help and direction (and you guessed it), had most of the money placed in a joint account with him. After he left (Yep! with the money), the uncle (the one with the IRS problems) sued Stephanie for the money.

Martha could have avoided the IRS with proper planning. Don't let your legacy be disrupted because you didn't take the time to create and execute your documents.

Probate Does Not Need to Be Feared

As we all know, probate is the legal process by which the deceased's assets are distributed after death. As simple as this sounds, we all have heard stories about how the assets were held up in probate for years. We have seen the drama spill out of our televisions as this celebrity or that person didn't have proper estate planning documents and everything ended up in probate for years.

What we don't hear about is the vast majority of estates that "sail" through probate with no issue at all. Probate need not be feared. It need not be avoided like the plague. It is not this dark hole that will suck everything down. Yes, the probate fees can be high (but usually aren't), and there is an infinite amount of time that the estate might be stuck in probate, but the vast majority of them have no problem at all and are settled usually around nine months or so.

If you think that your estate is going to be challenged by one of the heirs or by someone who thinks they *should* be an heir, well, that might be a reason to try to avoid probate. Mind you, that won't prevent the challenge. If you think creditors are looking for assets, if there are liens on the home, if there are other indications that assets are going to be attached after death, then you may wish to avoid probate. But, again, it won't prevent the creditors from coming.

> Jean just passed away sixteen months ago. She has two adopted children and named the oldest, her daughter, Nadia, to be the executrix. Nadia kept her brother informed of the assets and let him inspect as desired. The estate portion went through the probate process with the help of an attorney. Jean passed just a little over $2 million. There was no challenge. The debts and the taxes were all paid. Advertisements were bought, and trips were made back and forth to the court house. Nadia did most of the legwork, going here and there, while the attorney only performed the essential legal functions, and I helped with the financial transactions. There were no challenges, no problems, and everything went smoothly. The total fees were $7,500.

The bad news is by adding the kids to the deed, she gifted them part ownership.

> My mother passed away in 2000. She had five boys with five personalities. She named the oldest as executor, and everything, except her small IRA, was probated. No problem. No hassle. No challenge. Done.
>
> There are countless stories of probate with no problem. If you have prepared well, if you have identified well, if you have titled assets well, then there should be no problem for you either.

Be careful because there can be financial disasters by trying *too* hard to avoid probate.

> Samantha passed away in Seattle eighteen months ago. I am working with her daughter Danielle who has one brother. The will states "share and share evenly." The biggest asset is the home in

Seattle that Samantha and her father purchased fifty years ago. The home was worth about $400,000 at their mother's death and was purchased for $30,000. Like any home, Danielle tells me that it has its charm and has been well-maintained. When her husband died, Samantha received a step-up of his cost basis as normal.

Because she had heard of the negatives of probate, Samantha changed ownership of the home and added both of her children to the deed. By doing this, she did avoid probate, and by operation of law, the children became equal owners at her death. That is the good news.

The bad news is by adding the kids to the deed, she gifted them part ownership. Additionally, tax law says that if someone gifts an asset while alive, that asset is gifted with the original cost basis (how much was paid for it in the first place). Without realizing it, she gave them her original cost basis of fifty years ago. But, if you inherit after death, you get a step-up in cost basis. As the children tried to sell the property, they were faced with a down market. The property has not sold yet, but they will likely get about $350,000 for the house. If they had inherited the home, they would be looking at about a $50,000 capital loss (date of death value of $400,000 minus sale price of $350,000). Instead of being able to take a capital loss, Danielle and her brother will *each* pay a hefty capital gain tax based on the original (now gifted) cost basis!

We figured out that this tax is nearly *eight times* as much as probate would have cost.

As mentioned earlier, there are more concerns than going through the probate process. Don't be blinded by all of the negatives. You should only truly be worried if there is going to be a challenge of some kind.

——
We figured out that this tax is nearly eight times *as much as probate would have cost.*
——

11

NOTE: When there is a challenge against the estate, the judge will put the estate process on hold until the challenge is settled. Challenges come from all kinds of places, from family members who think they are owed more than what was given, to last-minute changes that cut someone out, to creditors who stake a claim against the estate.

You Will Never Be 100 Percent Certain

When you are creating your will and trust documents, you will most likely have a fairly good idea of where and how you want most of your assets to go. Be aware, there will always be some issue that nags at you. Consider the possibilities that one of your children might be getting divorced or perhaps someone in your husband's family has treated you very poorly since his passing that you are giving strong consideration to making a change. No matter what the issue is today, there will *always* be an issue. You will never be 100 percent certain as to the "where and how" your assets will transition.

Please don't let this prevent you from creating the documents in the first place. I have seen too many people delay the whole process because there were one or two issues that were not settled. Perhaps they were at 90 percent on all of the issues, but because of these smaller ones, they were paralyzed into doing nothing.

You are always able to amend your documents at any time. Move forward with creating your documents now and work on the smaller ten percent as they develop.

Write Out Your Wishes in Plain English

My recommendation when it comes to your estate planning documents is to write down in plain English what you want done with your money. How do you want it to be distributed and why? Who is getting what, and why? If you have a concern about a divorce, then mention it. If there is concern about how you are being treated, then write that down as well.

Let me give you an example of one family I know.

Stephen is the delightful son of a friend of mine. He enjoys life and is quickly identified as the happiest of my friend's children. Stephen has dimples to die for and when he smiles, he is one cute kid. With all Stephen's wonderful attributes, he struggles with connecting concepts and how they fit in the real world. My friend predicts that Stephen is going to be a car mechanic. He loves cars and will one day love to work on them and be pleased that someone will actually pay him to do so! If my friend and his wife die together, Stephen is the only one of their children who will receive a lifetime check and will not have any asset given outright to him.

You see, if all of a sudden he received his entire inheritance, they are certain that one of his "friends" will want to go to Las Vegas and help him spend it. Because it sounds like a great idea, Stephen would probably go and enjoy the heck out of himself. But when he comes back to town, he won't really understand why he has been fired from his job, why his friend is nowhere to be found, and why he has no money left.

They will write him a letter as to why they are making this decision and tell him he is loved dearly and that this decision is made to protect him. Without this explanation, perhaps he would not understand why his brother and sisters received their inheritance at once and he didn't.

By putting down your thoughts on paper, you can then sit down with a qualified estate planning attorney and have that attorney create the necessary legal documents and put these desires in force. You will also have a wonderful letter expressing your feelings for your family to forever cherish. Additionally, if there are any challenges to the estate, then this letter could be used to further illustrate what your true intentions were. Sometimes plain English is better than legal jargon!

Location of Your Important Papers

I have long recommended that you place a piece of paper in a Ziploc® bag and then place the bag in your refrigerator. On this paper, you should put directions and locations of all of your important estate planning documents, phone numbers, and such. One person asked me if the paper will get "freezer burn." I don't think so. In fact, it will be in a controlled temperature, low humidity environment and will never fade.

Why the refrigerator? If something happens to you and friends and family come in to care for you, they will all eventually go to the refrigerator to see what you have to eat! And if they have a special diet, they will buy their own food and put it there. Everybody knows where the refrigerator is, you can't misplace it, and you certainly can't hide it. Therefore, if your important documents are in there or at least the directions as to where they are, then no one will have to search to find them. Important directions and wishes will be found in a timely manner, and there will be no confusion as to your wishes.

*The easiest way for your children to learn about money
is for you not to have any.*

Katherine Whitehorn

Is Too Much Too Much?

There is beauty in the struggle and the sense of accomplishment. Great value is learned with the lessons of hard work, of being knocked down to pick yourself back up to keep moving toward a dream, and in the feeling of accomplishment of a job well done. As wealth is being transferred now like never before, there are many who are handed this wealth without the lessons of the struggle, being knocked down, the will to get back up, and the sweet taste of victory. Many today are downright spoiled rotten.

The U.S. Trust Survey of Affluent Americans, New York, 1996, with only the top 1 percent of affluent Americans being included, says it best. They concluded: "The wealthiest parents in the United States worry about the effects of affluence on their children and the notion that too much

Many today are downright spoiled rotten.

affluence can distort children's values and rob them of initiative. They are concerned that their children are grown up sheltered from the reality that it takes hard work to obtain affluence." This worry was true then and is true now.

When I was working at age sixteen in Firenze Restaurant in Shreveport, Louisiana, to put myself through private high school, I clearly remember a conversation around a large dining room table at Christmastime. As I was filling water glasses, I overheard a conversation about how many presents were under the tree, and the father said this to his son, "If you don't behave tonight, I'm going to take away present number twenty-six from you." Everyone at the table began to laugh. I remember that child never did behave. I don't begrudge the family their wealth. Personally, I am striving to achieve it myself. But I wonder whatever happened to him. Hopefully he wasn't a statistic, a teenager who had everything and ended up dead from an overdose or car crash.

Many years later when I lived in Florida, I heard a sad story about a sixteen-year-old boy who had just received his driver's license. His parents gave him the top-of-the-line brand new Mercedes Benz. On his very first night out, he took the curve way too fast, flipped the car several times, and died at the scene. Was that too much?

I heard recently that a multi-billionaire said that he was not going to give his entire fortune to his children. In fact, it appears that he is going to give the major portion of his wealth to charity and non-family members. I have heard (but don't consider the source necessarily reliable) that he is going to give his children each only about $1 billion! Huh? Is that too much?

May I recommend the book, *The Ultimate Gift* if you have significant wealth and need some guidance? May I also recommend that you *read* the book rather than watch the movie? [The movie is patently different than the book. I enjoyed reading about how a man tries to instill many gifts to his grandnephew and the lessons learned by the grandnephew along the way as he strives to earn the ultimate gift.]

As you consider passing your legacy, you may need to ask yourself if too much is too much. Instead of giving money to the family, perhaps you can give it to a foundation, have the family involved and teach them to give it to the community. There can be wonderful life lessons available to those willing to learn them.

Remember, you pass more than money.

What type of family harmony did she pass? What type of character did she leave her children? What was her legacy in the eyes of her offspring? Grandchildren?

———

Family Harmony

As you consider your financial plan and how assets are going to pass, you will need to consider that you pass more than money.

Throughout this book, we talk about mistakes that have been made including the idea that money is the only legacy we pass.

It always troubles me when I meet with clients and one of them says, "I will be gone, so I'll let them worry about it." This attitude is dangerous. It is not only money; it is your last statement to the world – your family and friends.

Be Careful if you Overweight One Child Over Another

It concerns me greatly when a client gives preferential treatment to one child over another. Normally the story sounds like this: "My two oldest children are doing well [either through hard work or because of their marriage], but the youngest is struggling. You see the oldest one started his own business [became a doctor, married a doctor] and the second one is in the military [has a steady job, always knows how to make money], but the youngest is in and out of trouble [has been married a couple of times, went to jail for a couple of years]. I am going to leave the youngest more money because he needs it more."

What does this say to the two successful children? Are they somehow devalued because of their success? Does their hard work and good fortune mean they are loved less? What about the youngest? By giving this child more money, does it reward the negative behavior? Does it enable this child to continue down a bad path?

I knew a family with two sons, Tom and Bill, in that order. Tom did well by himself. He put himself through college, became an engineer and was making a good living. He had a stable marriage with three children. Bill was the wayward one. He went to college but didn't graduate. Got married because his girlfriend was pregnant; the marriage didn't last. He worked low-paying manual labor type jobs and never seemed to earn enough. Bill fell into the wrong crowd and ended up trying to make a fast buck the illegal way. He went to jail for three years and came out none the better.

"He isn't a bad kid," his mother would say, and she was right. He wasn't really that bad. He just made bad decisions.

Every holiday the family would get together. Tom and his family would travel to his mother's home. Bill would always say, "Can't make it this year, don't have the money to get there." So Mom would pay his way. Mom always paid his way and never offered anything to Tom.

When their mother died, she made an uneven split in favor of Bill. What do you think her legacy is with her children? What did this type of decision mean to Tom and his family? Do you think there was harmony between the brothers?

The issue isn't the amount of money, but what the inheritance actually *says* about Mom. What type of family harmony did she pass? What type of character did she leave her children? What was her legacy in the eyes of her off spring? Grandchildren?

Second Marriage

Second marriages are very tricky when it comes to estate planning. If your husband passed away while you were young and you remarry, then you might have children from your second marriage, as well as your first. How do you treat the assets that you brought into the marriage? Do you set aside some of that money to your child from the first marriage? How does that impact your relationship with your husband and your new children? What if he brings children into the marriage?

Beth and Rick were married right out of college. David was born one year later, and when he was two, Rick was killed in a car crash. Luckily, he had prepared and there was adequate life insurance to care for the two of them. Eight years later, Beth remarried at age thirty-two. Steve was divorced from his wife, and he had two daughters. Together they had two children.

Beth told me that every time there is even a hint of the money that was left to David, Steve became very agitated. Beth told me, "This is the money that his dad left him."

Steve complained that he paid for all the expenses of the children from his first marriage, the children he had with Beth as well as David, even though David had his "own money" left to him by his biological father. The result is bitterness toward David.

This story is unfolding before my eyes. I am not sure how it is going to end up, but Beth is adamant about not spending any of David's money, except for David directly, and not for the other children. I have no predictions, but I fear it will not end well.

If you marry late in life, how are you going to treat your assets? What if your wealth is larger than his? Do you keep your money separate? Do you have it available for his benefit through a trust if you pass away first, in effect delaying the transfer to your children until he dies? Make sure you discuss these integral concerns about your family dynamics with your financial advisor and attorney. He or she can help you with important ideas and offer wisdom along the way.

Your Husband's Authority at Your Death

Many state laws grant strong authority to the surviving spouse at the passing of the other. You have to be rock certain that your wishes are clearly spelled out in your estate planning documents. If not, your new husband will decide where you are buried, what the headstone says, what kind of final service is conducted, and other details. If there is no will, the courts will generally defer to him over *your* adult children, and he will decide where your heirlooms go. Yes, he may have to pass a certain statutory dollar amount of your estate by intestate laws, but he doesn't have to pass your heirloom tea set or your jewelry. He can keep that for his family.

NOTE: Before the remarriage, give strong consideration to establishing a prenuptial agreement to establish ownership of certain heirlooms and important family possessions. Even if you have remarried and didn't do that, you can still create legal documents that will control your assets and dispose of them as you wish.

Your Family's Guiding Light^{SM}

Your Family's Guiding Light^{SM} is a wonderful booklet that provides your family written information about the facts in your life. Many families have discovered that talking about financial matters and estate planning issues to be more difficult than writing those matters down.

This valuable booklet allows you to identify areas of your life, that family members will need to know about, when the time comes that you will not be able to tell them yourself.

In one simple location, you will be able to instruct your loved ones on critically important matters, such as:

People to Contact
Legal Documents

Financial Accounting
On-Line Information and Passwords
Instructions for Survivors and Loved Ones

A close friend of mine went through what must be one of the toughest things to go through, he buried his daughter after a long battle of breast cancer after he had already buried his wife. Frank was in a terrible state. He knew that his daughter wanted certain college friends to be contacted at her death, and he knew that she had some particular songs she wanted played at the funeral.

But he *could not find* that information.

In the months after the funeral, while cleaning her room, he found that piece of paper with the friend's names and the song information (which was not sung).

Not only was he miserable about his daughter's death, but now he was tormented about not fulfilling her wishes.

From the booklet:

> "We all have the ability to leave a legacy of Love and Understanding. Or it can be one of angst and confusion. *Your Family's Guiding Light*SM will go a long way towards leaving the gift of Love and Understanding."

Once you fill your booklet out, let your family know that it exists, and where they can find it. Go here to order your booklet, in either hard copy or electronic delivery.

Thoughts

It's your legacy. You have the time to set it straight and to help pass what you truly intend to. The first ingredient is to know that you will leave a legacy. Now go create yours.

$\mathscr{R}$ecognizing the Need for a Plan

Productivity is never an accident.
It is always the result of a commitment to excellence, intelligent
planning, and focused effort.

Paul J. Meyer

Whether it is through death, divorce, or choosing to remain single, women have up to a ninety percent chance at some point in their lives of having to be solely responsible for their finances. Even in strong healthy marriages, many women need to take a greater interest in the household finances. Now, with the baby boomers moving toward retirement, the number of women who will find themselves financially alone is predicted to dramatically increase.

Unfortunately, women can be at a disadvantage. Call it culture or just being focused in different areas of life (raising children, being a wife, running a household, working), women are often not in a position to focus on financial matters or decisions. This doesn't mean that they *can't* make decisions; it means that in the world today, they may not have had the *opportunity* to make them. Often, when it finally becomes necessary for a woman to make financial decisions, she may not be fully prepared.

The best time to be fully prepared is not when you have been thrust into a situation where there is a large amount of money and you need to decide how to safeguard it. Many times, you now have this money because something negative happened, such as a death, divorce, or inheritance. Most people with instant money didn't win the lottery.

We all know it is challenging and often unwise to make financial decisions quickly and when under pressure (especially if you are newly widowed). Decisions made under pressure are often not the best ones, and mistakes can be made. When you make a small mistake with a small amount of money, the end result could be relatively painless, and there is often time to make up for the damage. If you make the same small mistake with a large amount of money, the result may be very painful. *And* recovering from the mistake takes longer.

To make matters worse, unscrupulous characters in the world – and in the financial industry – will gladly help you make bad financial decisions and help deplete you of your money.

Unique Challenges for Women

Women face many challenges in achieving a secure financial future, such as these:

- Although there are encouraging signs that the gap is closing, typically women earn less money than men.
- If her husband's job requires moving, a woman usually quits her job and starts a new one in the next location, often at a lower salary.
- Women often leave the workplace to raise children. Even if they return to work later, they save less money and generally have lower pensions and social security benefits.
- On average, women live seven years longer than men. This translates to seven more years of expenses, meals, clothes, and the like. If a husband were five years older than his wife, on average she will spend twelve years as a widow.
- Eighty to 90 percent of women will one day be solely responsible for their finances, primarily through death and divorce.
- In married households where there is more than $1 million in investable assets, over 40 percent of the women don't know where the finances are. (When I mention this to my clients, they remark, "I wouldn't be surprised if the number wasn't higher.")

Every tomorrow has two handles. You can take hold of the handle of anxiety or the handle of enthusiasm. Upon your choice, so will be your day.

Author Unknown

When you decide on having a dinner party, you need to select the menu. You usually have drinks and an appetizer, salad, main course, side dishes, and dessert. If you serve only one ingredient, such as lettuce, for the appetizer, the salad (not even dressing), the main course, and dessert, it not only would be strange, bland, and boring, but it would not encourage your guests to return for another dinner party.

A good party involves proper planning and offering a variety of choices as well as making some effort to engage your dinner guests. When you are talking about your finances, you must make a similar effort as well. You need to select your life's menu and create your financial plan.

Earlier, we discussed the importance of your plan and how it will speak to your heirs as your last statement when you die. Now we see why you must create a plan as you live. You may think of different ones but for me the three main reasons to create a financial plan are:

• Inflation
• Real Rates of Return
• Life Expectancy

Inflation

The most significant reason for planning your finances is to ensure that your money stays even with, and hopefully outpaces, inflation. Inflation is the silent killer of the value of money. Prices tend to go up over time. Your plan has to cover these increases. No matter how you received this money, the U.S. Post Office is not going to announce the following:

"Attention please, in light of the fact that (insert your name here) has received this money because of (insert reason here: death, inheritance, lottery, retirement, sale of assets), and in light of the fact that she is concerned about how to properly plan and really doesn't want to be bothered with creating a plan, be it hereby known that we therefore resolve to no longer raise the price of a stamp so she doesn't have to worry about inflation."

———

If you put all your money in the bank and delay creating a plan, you are indeed making *a decision and* starting *a plan.*

———

Of course this is very silly, but it certainly brings home the point. Financially, you have to at least keep your purchasing power and stay even with inflation. If you put all your money in the bank and delay creating a plan, you are indeed *making* a decision and *starting* a plan.

Inflation is the increase of the cost of goods and services. We recognize that things may cost more next year than now. This is expected for a strong economy that continually has increasing growth. Inflation has been very low in the last decade when compared to historical numbers but is likely to increase again.

Here we can see the impact inflation has had on stamps, homes and cars:

Brief history of the price of First Class Stamps[1]

| 1932 | 1978 | 1999 | 2007 | 20xx? |

National Average Sales Price to buy a single-family home

1934	$ 5,972[2]
1980	$ 76,400[2]
2000	$ 207,000[2]
2007	$ 313,000[2]
2013	$ 289,500[3]

Cost to buy a Buick automobile

1934	$ 925[3]
1980	$ 6,119[3]
2000	$ 15,834[4]
2007	$ 27,325[5]
2015	$ 36,390[6]

[1] US Postal Service
[2] www.census.gov/const/uspriceann.pdf
[3] www.thepeoplehistory.com
[4] www.historicalextarchive.com
[5] www.motortrend.com
[6] www.truecar.com/prices-new/buick

How much will these costs rise in ten years, in twenty years, or in thirty years?

You have to grow part of your money if you are going to keep even with inflation. Let's only hope that the hyperinflation that we had in the 1970's doesn't come back; such an event would make planning difficult. You have to make sure that when you create your financial menu, you have to have some ingredients that are designed to stay even with *and* outpace inflation.

---

*You have to
invest to beat
inflation and the
impact of taxes.*

Real Rates of Return

Not all investment choices will keep you even with or ahead of inflation. You have to invest to beat inflation and the impact of taxes. The real rate of return that I am talking about is (a) the growth of your money after you consider your tax bracket and (b) the increasing cost of goods and services (inflation). Remember, purchasing power is measured from your take-home money and its ability to purchase goods after the impact of inflation. So you have to keep taxes and inflation in mind when you calculate the real rate of return. Historically, the "easy" investments of CDs and other bank deposit accounts don't keep you even with inflation.

Let's take a look at the real rate of return and how different assets have performed in the twenty-year period from 1995 to 2014. *After* you factor in inflation the real rate of return each year would have been:

7.5%	3.8%	-1.3%
Stocks[1]	Bonds[2]	Cash[3]

[1]S&P 500 Index
[2]Barclay Total Bond Index
[3]J.P. Morgan Asset Management

When you add your personal tax bracket, the numbers become much worse. You may be shocked to find out that, over the last twenty years, holding money in cash actually *decreased* your purchasing power. Holding money in bonds kept you about even. With this in mind, let's look at the returns that you are getting on your checking or savings accounts at the bank.

According to www.bankrate.com, which watches daily rates across the nation, the average checking account in January, 2016 paid just 0.17 percent. A one-year CD paid 1.26 percent. The inflation average for 2014 clocked in at 1.62 percent.

You may be shocked to find out that, over the last twenty years, holding money in cash actually *decreased your purchasing power.*

Consider the following example as to why you can't just put money in the bank and think you have a proper long-term plan.

>If you deposited $100,000 into a "safe" CD paying 1.26 percent, at the end of the year, you would earn $1,260. In the 28 percent tax bracket, you would pay $352.80 in taxes, leaving you with $907.20 of interest and a total balance of $100,907.

>If inflation averaged around 1.62 percent, you would need $101,620 just to stay even with your purchasing power. Therefore, with your "safe" investment, you are $713 underwater! The savings account is much worse.

NOTE: Average inflation includes all Americans purchasing all goods -- from baby formula and diapers, to sports cars and club memberships, to medicine and walkers. *But*, if you look at those in retirement, and separate their goods and services from the rest, the inflation rate for medicine and walkers, entertainment trips, and items those in retirement are purchasing, their inflation rate is higher than the average! This makes the need to stay level and outpace "retirement inflation" even greater.

Life Expectancy

The final reason why creating your financial recipe is so important is that our average life expectancy is getting longer and longer. The price of a stamp is not going to go down and neither will the cost of goods and services. You have to use the ingredients you have been given and create a financial recipe that anticipates your increasing longevity. You have to prepare to keep even or ahead of inflation.

I have said it before and will say it again: "You don't want to be an old lady on a fixed income." You have to create a growth plan for life! If you have only traditional bank deposits (CDs, checking, savings, money market accounts), you *are* on a fixed income.

Flip to the back of the book under Charts and Tables, page 189 and find the Actuarial Chart. Often, I will hear someone say, "I am sixty years old and I am now on my own. I don't want to take any risk and I

> *Without comprehensive planning, there actually is no real plan at all.*

don't have time to *play* in the stock market." If you look at the chart, the average life expectancy for a sixty-year-old woman is 24.37 more years. This means that there is a 50 percent chance that she will live *longer* than 24.37 more years. If she puts money she just received (either due to death or divorce) in bank deposit accounts, she will quickly lose purchasing power and be in trouble in years to come.

Remember, these deposit accounts are great ingredients. They are sound and often FDIC insured. But like any recipe, if all you have is one ingredient, you don't have a meal; you just have a lot of one ingredient. You will see coming up in chapter 5 where deposit items work very well.

Three Mistakes the Wealthy Make

Gather, don't scatter.

Over the years investors have been convinced that proper investing meant taking their money and spreading it out amongst several investment professionals. Over time, many investors accumulate, on average, four advisors and several accounts. From his 401(k), Roth IRA, Traditional IRA, brokerage and mutual fund accounts, to her 401(k), Traditional IRA, trust and saving accounts, a family can accumulate several accounts with several financial institutions.

This scattering of assets leads to a false sense of "diversification" by "not putting all of your eggs in one basket." Trouble is, this strategy really hurts most investors.

Many investors have unknowingly scattered their assets, resulting in no one person managing or fully understanding their entire situation, goals or dreams. Without comprehensive planning, there actually is no plan at all.

1. Improper Asset Allocation

Most clients come to me with their assets dispersed with several advisors and several financial firms. No single advisor knows what the other is doing resulting in an uncoordinated portfolio. One advisor in firm A might be selling the very asset that an advisor in firm B is buying. Unless there is one coach reviewing the entire portfolio, then your money is not coordinated.

Your asset allocation should always reflect your current position in life, your current goals, future, feelings and family characteristics. When your hard earned money is scattered to other advisors and institutions, only you are left to properly manage your portfolio. Many individuals are not trained to monitor this correctly and consistently. Unfortunately, the overall plan suffers.

2. Improper Correlation Within Investments, Managers and Funds

Without it saying, each investment needs to be excellent on its own. The investment, manager or mutual fund needs to have a strong track record (I like a ten-year record). You might be able to select quality investments. That's not the problem. Where the breakdown occurs is knowing how these investments interrelate. This is nearly impossible to track when one advisor is doing one thing, and a different advisor is doing just the opposite.

Let's think about a recipe analogy. You might have the best ingredients to make your favorite dish. You might even have quality chefs at your beck and call ready to make this dish for you. If you put all of these chefs in the same kitchen but don't let them know what the other is doing, a culinary disaster awaits. You can see that the likelihood of your dish coming out correctly is very low, no matter how good the ingredients were. Same is true with your investment portfolio.

3. Failure to Monitor the Consolidated Portfolio

You know life is not static. Life is constantly changing. Whether it's your job, children, the economy, world events, new laws, unplanned expenses (and the list goes on and on), your world constantly moves. Your entire portfolio needs to be dynamic as well. When market forces move, the properly managed portfolio needs to move with it. I am not talking about day-trading, but rebalancing when and where appropriate. Additionally, your goals, future, feelings and family characteristics are changing as well. Every day is either a day closer to your goals, or not.

Having your assets scattered makes it nearly impossible to properly monitor your portfolio based on your changing life. With the technology and tools available, along with the new "open architecture" available at full service financial institutions, you are better off hiring one advisor to help you monitor your portfolio. This trusted advisor will coordinate all of your "eggs" and not put them in the same "basket." He/she can manage your diversified portfolio to meet your goals, future, feelings and family characteristics and make sure your entire portfolio works in unison to make your dreams come true.

NOTE: In the past, many firms were limited to the solutions they could individually bring to the client. Many had their own proprietary funds or investments, which may or may not have been in your best interest. Today, full service firms have an "open architecture" and are able to go out into the market place and bring any solution to you that is appropriate. For your strong consideration, only hire an advisor who can go anywhere in the marketplace without limitation!

Thoughts

You have many good years ahead of you. My wish is that while you are alive, you live. Take a look at the life expectancy chart. As we become healthier and medicine gets even better, life expectancy is increasing. I bet you have longer to live than a short-term financial plan will support.

Why bother? Because if you don't, your lifestyle will be compromised by inflation that will erode your purchasing power.

---

*I bet you have
longer to live
than a short-term
financial plan will
support.*

3

Evaluating Your Wants, Needs, Goals, and Dreams

The great decisions of human life usually have far more to do with the instincts and other mysterious unconscious factors than with conscious will and well-meaning reasonableness. The shoe that fits one person pinches another; there is no universal recipe for living. Each of us carries his own life-form within him—an irrational form which no other can outbid.

Jean Baudrillard

Any recipe has to start with some fundamental questions: Is this for breakfast, lunch, or dinner? Meat, fish, vegetarian? Salad, soup, antipasto? Bread, wheat, rye, multi-grain? And many other considerations come into question before you start pulling out the ingredients. The same is true with your life's financial recipe.

Where do you start? Many times clients will come in with money available to invest and ask me, "What is the best recommendation that you can make for this money?" Without any further information, any answer from me would be malpractice. There is not nearly enough information yet. For me to give an honest response, I must know the client's goals, in other words, what's the ultimate recipe you are trying to create? Then I can choose the ingredients. So we have to start with important questions.

As you create your plan, you need to consider the following simple, yet powerful, three questions:

1. What are your life goals?
2. How much money do you need to keep in emergency cash in order to feel comfortable and sleep at night?
3. What are your known extra expenses between now and the next four years or so?

What Are Your Life Goals?

Paint a color picture of how your life, including retirement, will look. Depending on your life's circumstances, you may have a goal of traveling, spending time with family, or getting that sailboat that you always dreamed about. If you are reading this book and you are now widowed, your goals and dreams didn't die with your husband. In fact, the best way for you to live is to keep your goals and dreams alive.

What are they? Spend some time writing them down and forecasting what it is that you want to do.

Do you know what the difference between a goal and a dream is? Napoleon Hill (no relation) answered in the following simple yet profound way:

A goal is a dream with a deadline.

Review your list of goals and dreams and put an "accomplish by" date beside each entry.

Most goals should be practical goals, but some can be "stretch" goals. Consider even the most outrageous goal, one that you would love to accomplish. Even if you feel that you don't have the ability to accomplish it, put it down. That goal will help you move forward with the rest.

Review your list of goals and dreams and put an "accomplish by" date beside each entry.

How Much Emergency Cash Do You Need in Order to Feel Comfortable?

Now that you have your goals identified, the next question to be answered when you start creating your financial plan is this one about emergency cash. You need to consider your circumstances to help you come up with a reasonable amount.

Some experts in the field suggest that you have cash to cover at least three to nine months of living expenses. While this is a great place to start, you must also consider such things as where your extended family lives.

> Helga's family lives in Germany. If she received an emergency call to come home, she would have to be on a last-minute international flight and potentially have to rent a car, stay in a hotel, and shoulder a number of non-discounted expenses. I encouraged her to have more cash than the normal three to nine months of living expenses. If your family is within driving distance, you may need to keep less.

If you are in your working years and your skill is very marketable and you are willing to move if needed, then you probably only need three months. If, on the other hand, your income is unpredictable or from less secure resources, you may need cash for nine months of expenses. Additionally, if you are not marketable in the workplace, or you are generally unwilling or unable to move, and you may need to "wait it out" for a while, then I would have cash for at least nine months of expenses.

Another consideration is your lifestyle. If you have a gardener and pool service, there is a big difference than if you live in a small apartment.

> Steve and Sally have strong income and a nice home. They have four girls in college. Sally told me she wants $100,000 in emergency cash "because you never know what the girls might need."

Emergency cash money should be very liquid and readily available. An interest-paying money market is typically a perfect place to keep your emergency cash. No, you won't earn a lot of interest on this money, but it will be available without penalty or loss if and when needed. As your emergency either happens or not, work with your advisor to adjust the amount that you need. Keeping too much money in cash or CDs will be a drag on your well-thought-out financial plan.

What Are Your Known Extra Expenses Between Now and the Next Four Years or So?

Once you've determined how much emergency cash you need to keep available, the next consideration is this:

"In the next four years or so, what expenses do you know are coming up?"

This question does not refer to day-to-day expenses such as your grocery, electric, or mortgage payments. You know about those and they're generally covered with cash flow. I am talking about your other known "extra" expenses you have coming up over the next four or so years.

For example, do you plan on buying a boat? A plane? A new car? Are you going to go on a vacation around the world in eighty days? Do you plan to put children (grandchildren) through college? What are your normal vacation plans? Do your house need a new roof?

When you identify these expenses, write them down by category and place a reasonable dollar amount beside them. Be fair with the price and avoid under or over budgeting.

Plan how you are going to pay for these expenses. If you are working or you have a strong cash flow, you may be able to pay for these extras from your income. On the other hand, if you are not working and perhaps are already retired, then you may need to plunk this money down in anticipation of this upcoming expense.

Let me give you an example:

Ethel came to me at age seventy-two and had no financial plan. She was widowed and had already retired and could not generate extra money from her cash flow. After setting aside her emergency cash, she told me that one of her dreams was that when she turns seventy-five, she wants to take her whole family on a seven-night cruise to celebrate this birthday milestone. What a great dream! [In reality, this is a goal because it has a built-in deadline.]

The first question I asked her was if she would be willing to adopt me to be a part of her family. She laughed and said no. I then asked how many passengers and how much per passenger. "Seventeen passengers," she pronounced, that included a couple of brothers and sisters, her children and their spouses, and all her grandchildren. The price per passenger she said was $3,000.

17 passengers at $3,000 per passenger = $51,000 total

The only prudent thing we could do with this $51,000 known extra expense was buy a two-and-a-half-year CD. When Ethel reaches seventy-four-and-a-half, this CD will come due. She's going to go on her seven-night cruise!

Footnote: She thinks I'm a hero! You see, she purchased this CD in year 2000 when the markets were still heading straight up. Other advisors had suggested she put this money in a mutual fund so she could grow the money. Every investment should match your goal. Ethel needed funds at a certain date in the future and needed to invest accordingly to make certain those funds were available at that date. If the principle of investing was violated and she invested in a longer term investment, such as a mutual fund, then history tells us that a mutual fund decision would have negatively impacted her plan. She would have had to leave some of her family on the shore, or she would have had to cut the trip from seven nights to maybe three.

You have *your* goals and dreams written down. Identify the amount of your emergency cash that will keep you comfortable and able to sleep at night. You also have to identity your known extras coming up. Once you do that, it is now time to create a long-term financial plan.

Let's Put Some Numbers Down

Considering the concepts of emergency cash and known extras, we can start putting some numbers down. The best way to illustrate the creation of a plan is to talk with you about Mary.

> Mary's husband passed away, and from his estate, life insurance, and other assets, she had $500,000 in cash and investments. After considering the first question, Mary determined that her emergency cash need was $40,000.
>
> We then looked at her known extra expenses from now to the next four or so years. She said that she would need a new car; she wanted to do some traveling; the house would need a new roof; and she wanted to give a memorial donation to the church. We wrote these down and her list looked like this:

New car	$ 30,000 (in about eighteen months)
Vacations	$ 8,000 ($2,000 a year for four years)
New roof	$ 17,000 (in three years)
Memorial to church	$ 5,000 (in six months)
Total of Known Extras	$ 60,000

From here, it is simple math.

$500,000 available
- $ 40,000 emergency cash to let you sleep well at night
- $ 60,000 known expenses placed in short-term ingredients
$400,000 available for longer term planning

Reflection

Depending on your current age, you may be thinking that $400,000 has to be invested in something that is guaranteed. The problem with this thinking is "guaranteed" ingredients are not designed to outpace inflation.

I have had many people come to me - married men and women who are in their sixties - who believe, "We are too old to be playing the stock market. Just put us in CDs." Part of their thinking is correct. Everybody is too old to "play" the market. But they are certainly young enough to still need to grow their money. I heard it said that a married sixty-five year-old couple who are healthy nonsmokers have a 58 percent chance that one of them will live to be ninety years old. That's twenty-five years from now. Twenty-five years is *not* a short amount of time.

As you create your life's recipe, you need to create the plan as if you were going to live long (and statistics show you are going to live much longer than you think).

> If you plan to live long and sadly you live short, that would be unfortunate. However, if you planned your money to live short and you lived long, that would be a travesty!

Spend a moment with me and look back just twenty years. According to www.1990sflashback.com, here is what we see:

	1995	2015
President	Bill Clinton	Barack Obama
Vice President	Al Gore	Joe Biden
U.S. Population is*	226,764,948	322,765,840
Life expectancy is**	75.8 years	79.3 years
Dow Jones Industrial Average	5,118	17,425
Inflation***	2.5%	0.50%
Cost of a new home	$158,500	$289,500
Median household income	$34,076	$53,836
Price of a gallon of regular gas	$1.15	$2.09
Price of a first-class stamp	$0.32	$0.49
Cost of a dozen eggs	$1.16	$1.66
Cost of a gallon of milk	$2.96	$3.86

Source: www.1990sflashback.com/1995/Economy.asp
*As of 1/1/2016 according to http://www.census.gov/main/www/popclock.html
**www.data360.org/dsg.aspx?Data_Set_Group_Id=195
***www.inflationdata.com

The point is evident. What are the next twenty years going to look like? How will you be prepared? Would you rather plan to live over those next twenty years with a well-thought-out plan or just take it six months at a time? We should financially prepare ourselves for it! You need to create your *recipe for living, a recipe for life*.

Thoughts

Make sure that you take some time to evaluate your wants, needs, goals and dreams. They may be much different than what you thought they might be. For me, this is one of the most important ingredients that a client can bring to our discussions. Knowing what you want will help me plan for you to achieve it.

The problem with this thinking is ingredients that are "guaranteed" are not designed to grow.

4

Courage For the Journey

*Obstacles are those frightful things you see when you
take your eyes off your goal.*

Henry Ford

As you move forward, one of the most important aspects of creating your recipe is to fully understand your risk tolerance and your willingness to place your money in areas that have growth potential. Do not underestimate your need to take some risk and the value of taking risk. Conversely, don't take on too much risk. Don't become a *gambler* instead of a *planner*.

Too many times I hear, "I can't afford to take risk. I can't afford to lose any money. I am too old to be in the stock market." My comment back is: "You can't afford not to take *some* risk."

The risk you take should not be the "close your eyes and just pick a stock" risk. That would be crazy risk. You should take the type of risk I refer to as controlled risk.

Controlled Risk

*Don't become a
gambler instead
of a planner.*

Let me give you an example of controlled risk. Let's say that you have your favorite recipe put together. You have prepared the ingredients, mixed as instructed, and placed your creation in the baking dish. The directions call for a preheated oven and then bake for thirty minutes. Well, you are turning on the heat, essentially taking these raw ingredients and subjecting them to hundreds of degrees. This is mighty risky and dangerous. What if you leave your recipe in too long? Or not long enough? What if the temperature control breaks and the oven overheats, or under heats? What if you put something other than cooking ingredients into the oven? Paper would catch on fire. Crayons and candles would melt. Clothes wouldn't dry; they'd catch fire.

Every time you turn on your oven, you are *intentionally* starting a fire in your kitchen.

You may never have thought about it, but your ingredients need controlled heat in order to cook. Well, so do your investments. You need to expose them to controlled risk. You don't want to overcook your investments. You don't want them to be undercooked either.

> *Every time you turn on your oven, you are* intentionally *starting a fire in your kitchen.*

Crazy Risk

As much as we have controlled risk in many things we do (without even thinking about it), we are also subject to crazy risk. Consider a bottle of medicine your doctor prescribed. You know that if you take one pill a day for two weeks, your ailment will go away.

However, if you misuse the medicine and consume the entire bottle at once and in full, you will likely overdose.

Abusing medicine would be crazy risk. The same goes with speeding at night in a blizzard. And jumping off the high dive (or low dive for that matter) when there is no water in the pool.

It is easy to see that controlled risk helps us enjoy life and misusing everyday items potentially leads us to disaster.

Investment risk is the same. With controlled risk and using the market as it was intended to be used, you will likely achieve your long term goals and dreams.

Yes, it is very comfortable to bring all of your money to the bank and buy CDs. But as comfortable as that is, you may be headed for disaster. Buying short-term, non-growth CDs that won't keep up with inflation is really not part of a well-thought-out strategy for a long-term plan. You have to expose some of your money to controlled risk and work to stay even with and hopefully outpace inflation.

Risk Tolerance of Your Ingredients

One of the biggest overlooked areas of creating a financial plan is properly determining your risk tolerance. When the markets are doing well, everybody has a high tolerance for risk. When they are doing poorly, everybody becomes risk averse. Most likely, the answer for you is somewhere in the middle.

Women (and men) who are facing financial issues alone do not feel comfortable with risk. They are content with keeping all their assets in depository type products that are FDIC insured. This is the most comfortable and easy choice.

Unfortunately, this choice is made too often (remember my own mother made this one) and starts you down the path to becoming "an old lady on a fixed income." So what is the alternative? You have to grow some of the money. It doesn't have to be high-risk growth; it doesn't have to be dot.com growth. It should be growth nonetheless.

Even if you are sixty years old, your life expectancy is over twenty years! You can't afford not to have some money growing. And the reason you need the growth is because the cost of everything you buy is growing (inflation), and if you are going to keep up with this growth, you need to have a plan.

Your investment portfolio is like a large garden. When you are younger, you have to sow the seeds that will grow. Your garden is just bare land. With solid investments, you will see your garden starting to grow—a growth that will withstand all types of weather and natural occurrences. Yes, there might be a section of your garden that gets wiped out in a rainstorm, but over time you will have solid growth.

Big solid companies are what I am referring to when I suggest exposing your money to growth, not the dot.com companies.

As you move into retirement, you will need to harvest those investments. You will turn your garden into income, to supplement retirement. As you harvest one section of the garden, you still need to plant new seeds and grow another section. Just like your garden's assets, your financial assets should have the benefits of growth. No matter the age you are right now, think how your finances would be different, and substantially better, if twenty years ago you invested in Home Depot, Wal-Mart, Coca-Cola, ConocoPhillips, Microsoft, McDonald's, Johnson & Johnson, Procter & Gamble, and Campbell Soup[1], just to name a few. Big solid companies are what I am referring to when I suggest exposing your money to growth, not the dot.com companies. No one can guarantee the future, but owning shares of stock in big solid companies should be part of the plan.

Included here is a Risk Analysis Questionnaire with which you may wish to take and score.

Here's how it works:

Questions one through five measure your attitude toward and your willingness to accept risk. Question six measures your years until you expect to spend the money. Remember, this is not when you might *begin* an income stream, but this is when you plan on cashing out and taking the proceeds to buy something. For example, you have to start withdrawing from your IRA at age seventy-and-a-half, but you might not have any plans to totally cash out. If you are now age sixty-five, you would *not* say that you have five years to go. In reality, you would have the rest of your life, hopefully greater than twenty years!

By understanding the risk, we can better prepare how to create a financial recipe that will work with your risk level, help you maintain your lifestyle and help you to outpace inflation.

---

[1]This is not a recommendation to buy. Consult with your advisor to see if these or other investments are appropriate for your long term plan.

Risk Analysis Questionnaire

1. I will risk some safety in an attempt to stay ahead of inflation.

Agree	4 points	
Somewhat Agree	3 points	
Somewhat Disagree	2 points	_____
Disagree	1 point	score

2. I will risk some safety for potentially higher returns.

Agree	4 points	
Somewhat Agree	3 points	
Somewhat Disagree	2 points	_____
Disagree	1 point	score

3. I know the market can go down; I am willing to accept negative returns.

Agree	4 points	
Somewhat Agree	3 points	
Somewhat Disagree	2 points	_____
Disagree	1 point	score

4. I will accept fluctuating returns in order to potentially achieve my goal.

Agree	4 points	
Somewhat Agree	3 points	
Somewhat Disagree	2 points	_____
Disagree	1 point	score

5. I will accept greater volatility to potentially achieve greater returns.

Agree	4 points	
Somewhat Agree	3 points	
Somewhat Disagree	2 points	_____
Disagree	1 point	score

Now add up the score for your total points and place the number here:

_____

Total Risk Score

6. In approximately how many years do you expect to need the money you are investing?

3 years	1 point
5 years	2 points
10 years	3 points
15 years	4 points
20 years	5 points
Greater than 20 years	6 points

Put that score here for your Time Horizon _____

Time Horizon

On the next page, score yourself to identify your potential allocation.

Take the time horizon score and circle the appropriate number <u>across the top.</u> Then, take the total risk score and circle it along the <u>left side</u>. Find the corresponding box for your potential risk allocation.

Time Horizon

Risk Score	1	2	3	4	5	6
5	Conservative	Conservative	Conservative	Conservative	Conservative	Conservative
6	Conservative	Conservative	Conservative	Conservative	Conservative	Conservative
7	Conservative	Conservative	Conservative	Mod Conserv	Mod Conserv	Mod Conserv
8	Conservative	Conservative	Mod Conserv	Mod Conserv	Mod Conserv	Mod Conserv
9	Conservative	Conservative	Mod Conserv	Mod Conserv	Mod Conserv	Mod Conserv
10	Conservative	Mod Conserv	Mod Conserv	Mod Conserv	Mod Conserv	Moderate
11	Conservative	Mod Conserv	Mod Conserv	Mod Conserv	Mod Conserv	Moderate
12	Mod Conserv	Mod Conserv	Moderate	Moderate	Moderate	Moderate
13	Mod Conserv	Mod Conserv	Moderate	Moderate	Moderate	Mod Aggressive
14	Mod Conserv	Mod Conserv	Moderate	Moderate	Moderate	Mod Aggressive
15	Mod Conserv	Mod Conserv	Moderate	Mod Aggressive	Mod Aggressive	Mod Aggressive
16	Mod Conserv	Mod Conserv	Mod Aggressive	Mod Aggressive	Mod Aggressive	Mod Aggressive
17	Mod Conserv	Mod Conserv	Mod Aggressive	Mod Aggressive	Mod Aggressive	Aggressive
18	Mod Conserv	Moderate	Mod Aggressive	Mod Aggressive	Aggressive	Aggressive
19	Mod Conserv	Moderate	Mod Aggressive	Aggressive	Aggressive	Aggressive
20	Mod Conserv	Moderate	Mod Aggressive	Aggressive	Aggressive	Aggressive

Stock / Bond	
20/80	Conservative
40/60	Mod Conserv (Moderate Conservative)
50/50	Moderate
60/40	Mod Aggressive (Moderate Aggressive)
80/20	Aggressive

45

This broad risk score should be the basis of starting to create your plan. If you scored 'conservative' you may wish to consider a 20% stock and an 80% bond portfolio. See here the other outcomes to your score.

REMINDER: This stock to bond mix is only for the investable portion of your portfolio and does not include your emergency cash or known extras.

Stock Market Ingredients Are Volatile

We all know that the stock market has volatility. One day it is up, the next down, then the next way up, and so forth. Can't it just go up smoothly? Why does the market move like this?

Let me ask a simple question:

What makes a company's stock price go up in the long run?

Many will answer supply and demand. I say no. Some will answer excellent management. I say no. How about the quality of the product or the service? Still, no. Yes, I think those are contributing factors and part of the answer. But the only answer that matters is this.

The company's ability to increase its value by earning a profit.

NOTE: There are many contributing factors to a company's stock price, to be sure, but here I want to break down to the fundamental core as to why I believe over time, the company's stock price will go up.

Profit! That's it. It is no more complicated than that.

You see, there could be limited supply and great demand for the product, but if you can only sell it at a loss, then there is no profit. You will go out of business.

You could have great management and the ability to motivate people, but if the product can't be sold at a profit, then the company will lose money and close.

Even the quality of the product could be top-flight, the best ever made, but if it can't be sold at a profit, then it is of no use. Think of the now defunct eight-track tape. You could have the best one ever made, no defects, perfect condition, best quality ever, and produced by the best management team ever. But if there is no market and no one willing to buy it, you have no ability to earn a profit.

If the company can conceive of an idea, manufacture the product, package it, put it on a truck, ship it to a store, put it on a shelf, and sell it for a *profit*, then it doesn't matter what "it" is. The value of the company will go up. "It" could be oil flowing through a pipeline, caramel carbonated syrup inside of a soda pop can, or medicine inside of a bottle. If the company can conceive of the idea and sell it for a profit, then the stock price will tend to go up over time.

Now we know about the long run, so here is the next question:

What makes a company's stock price (and the whole market for that matter) fluctuate in the short run?

Answer: *short-term emotion resulting from short-term conditions.*

For example, remember Hurricane Katrina in August of 2005? As it was picking up steam in the Gulf of Mexico, wide speculation of potential damage to the oil platforms caused a run-up in oil futures, leading to higher gas prices. Then when Hurricane Rita came threatening Houston, Texas, this only added to emotional hype. Neither hurricane actually caused measurable oil damage, thus no disruption of the ability to earn a profit, but there were wide movements of the price, all based on emotion from short term conditions.

Another example is all of the dot.coms. Strong emotions of a "new economy" led to exaggerated prices on companies, especially if they had a Web site ending with a ".com" address. Prices were being bid up so high that the name of the game was not based on the ability to earn a profit (most of them never did), but on the bet that someone else would be willing to pay an even higher price on the emotions and hope that *someday* there would be a profit. When the emotion ended and profit was demanded (and not obtained), the bubble burst and prices collapsed.

Yet, in the long run, if any of these and other companies have the ability to earn a profit, their value and that of their stock will appreciate and go up.

This simple concept is important as you create your diversified portfolio. The market volatility needs to be understood and appreciated for what it is, but it should not be feared.

When the emotion ended and profit was demanded (and not obtained). the bubble burst and prices collapsed.

Accept Fluctuations and Start Investing Today

If you expect to continue to purchase stocks throughout your lifetime, you should welcome price declines as a way to add stocks more cheaply to your portfolio.

Warren Buffett

Yes, the market is volatile and fluctuates with the emotion of the day. You have to resist this short-term emotional concern. You see, if the economy as we know it continues, I believe the stock market has to go up over time. [I first wrote this sentence in early 2009 when the market was at 8,072. As of this writing, it is at 17,553. Over double in seven years.]

What has to be realized is before you can invest in the market, you need to use only that portion of your portfolio that has time to "cook" in the market. The money you invest in the stock market should not be needed in the short term. Historically, if money can be there five or more years, you have a wonderful chance of coming out with a profit.

Consider the following historical data on the well-known Investment Company of America (ICA) mutual fund.[1] From January 1, 1934 through December 31, 2014, there were eighty-one one year periods. For example, from start of year 1934 to end of year 1934, this is one period. In the same way, from start of year 1970 to end of year 1972, this is a three year period. So for my discussion here, one period is the beginning of one year through the end of that year. A three year period is the beginning of one year and held for three complete years. If you had invested your money in ICA and reinvested the dividends, you would have had the following chances of making money:

	Positive Results	Negative Results
If you held for only one year period	67%	33%
If you held for a three year period	86%	14%
If you held for a five year period	92%	8%
If you held for a ten year period	100%	0%

To better explain this chart, let's recap. There are eighty-one years of investing from 1934 to the end of 2014. If you held for three consecutive years, there are seventy-nine rolling three-year periods and eighty-six of them were positive. If you held for a ten-year period, there are seventy-two rolling periods and *all* ten years were positive.

To say it differently, if you only had one year to investment money, you would have a 67% chance to have more money at the end of your year. But if you held it for three years, you would increase your chances to 86%.

Of course the future is unknown, but if companies continue to earn a profit and you have time to invest a portion of your portfolio, you have exciting odds to be able to come out ahead.

Market Timing

In any given year, the market goes up and down. Many clients will tell me when the market is high, that the market is "too high" to invest. Then, when the market slows down during the year, they will say it is "going even lower, can't invest now."

Well, for me the best time to invest is when you have the money. No one is smart enough to "time" the market. But what if you could? Wouldn't that be great?

Of course, at some point in every year there is a market "high" and a market "low." If you invested on the market high, that would be the worst day of the year to invest. The best day to invest would be at the market low.

In the Chart and Tables section are the annual figures, but if you let me, I will summarize here the results.

Over the twenty years from 1995 through 2014, which as you know included the 9/11/01 attacks and recently the stock market crash of the 2008-2009 period, if you had invested $10,000 every year for twenty years in the Dow Jones Industrial Average** (DJIA):

- On the worst day (market high for that year) you would have $431,620, a 7.3 percent on average yearly return.***
- On the best day (market low for that year) you would have $542,140, a 9.0 percent on average yearly return.***
- And if you had invested in one-year CDs that rolled over, you would have $254,530, a 3.16 percent return.***

Worst Day Results (Market High)	Best Day Results (Market Low)	CDs being reinvested
$431,618	$542,138	$254,530

NOTE: There is no consideration for taxes or dividends. If dividends were reinvested, the returns would be even higher.

NOTE: As you add to a stock portfolio, you are not selling any of the stocks you had the year before. The ongoing tax consequence results only from dividends received as there are no capital gains until sold. However, when your CD comes due, each and every year you pay taxes on the interest received, therefore you actually roll into the next year your interest *less* your taxes you have to pay.

Thoughts

When you compared the returns from a stock portfolio made up of stocks from the Dow, to returns from investments in CDs, there really is no comparison.

You will never be able to time the market. You will sometimes invest on the best day to invest, and sometimes on the worst. Most of the time, you will invest somewhere in the middle. If my personal results are somewhere in the middle, I will be successful over the long run.

* The Standard and Poors 500 Index is a broad-based measure of 500 U.S. stocks and includes the reinvestment of dividends. The general public can not invest directly in the S&P Index. Data is actual performance of the S&P 500 Index and does not reflect future results.

** The Dow Jones Industrial Average (DJIA or commonly called the Dow) is a stock market index that measures the price of only thirty of the largest and most widely held U.S. public companies as a way to gauge the strength of the U.S. market.

*** See chart in Charts and Tables section, pages 190-192 to see the year by year calculations for the DOW and the CDs

[1] ICA Guide 2015

When you compared the returns from a stock portfolio made up of stocks from the Dow, to returns from investments in CDs, there really is no comparison.

$\mathcal{I}$nvestments

Investing should be more like watching paint dry or watching grass grow. If you want excitement, take $800 and go to Las Vegas.
                                                            Paul Samuelson

Your plan for living and your plan for life need to start first with the consideration of your life's goals, then your need for emergency cash. After that, you need to allocate for known extras that are expected and anticipated in the next several years.

Because you have allocated emergency cash and you have considered how to pay for your known extras, you now have the opportunity to build your plan for longer term growth. If the market crashes, no problem. Your emergency (that hopefully never comes) is covered, and your known extras (vacations, car, new roof) are already planned and allocated for.

Kim is divorced at age sixty. She has a life expectancy of twenty-three more years. She cannot afford to be without some growth. Even though her children are well meaning, she cannot put all her money in the bank. She said, "They just want me to put my money in CDs." After looking at her other assets, which included her IRA, half of Roger's 401(k), and half of the joint account, we coordinated the whole portfolio to meet her growth needs *without* taking any undue risk.

Investment Pyramid and Time Line

Take a look at the Investment Pyramid illustrated here. This is a standard investment pyramid that you may have seen before. You will see that it is divided into five equal sections. At the bottom of the pyramid is where there is no short-term risk and the top is the most risky. (We will talk about the definitions of risk in depth in Part Two, *Asset Classes.*)

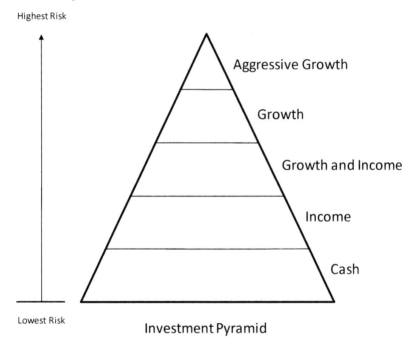

Highest Risk

Aggressive Growth

Growth

Growth and Income

Income

Cash

Lowest Risk

Investment Pyramid

Start at the bottom and work your way up.

Cash is king. Yes, but it doesn't multiply if it is not put to use. In the short run, it is very comfortable. Let's say you have a $100 bill in your pocket. If the market crashes, no problem, you still have your money. The problem in the long run is you still have that $100, and it is now worth less (because of inflation). In the long run, you have been hurt by your $100 bill because cash doesn't grow.

Moving up the pyramid you see the *Income* category. This is not income that you earn, but income that your money earns. In this category, we find bonds and other investments primarily focused on generating cash. It might be very comfortable to put the majority of our assets here. However, bonds are not designed to grow; a $100,000 bond years later at maturity is still worth $100,000 (with less purchasing power – because of inflation). Putting assets only here may result in becoming an old lady on a fixed income. You find interest-bearing investments here, like CDs and bonds (even bond mutual funds). We have already learned that CDs and bonds don't generally keep up with inflation.

> *The problem in the long run is you still have $100,000 and it is now worth less (because of inflation).*

The *Growth and Income* risk category is what I consider the "sweet spot" in investing. This category is where you find utility companies, companies that historically pay strong dividends, all the while giving you some growth potential. Yes, the stock prices in this category do and will fluctuate, but the up and down ride is not as shocking and has over time outpaced inflation.

> *The Growth and Income risk category is what I call the "sweet spot" in investing.*

The *Growth* risk category is next representing companies that are on the move. Many of these companies are still expanding and growing into different markets. Companies like Wal-Mart, Home Depot, and Coca-Cola are still growing and looking for growth opportunities. Many growth companies are now looking beyond U.S. borders to find international consumers. This category will fluctuate more as the market moves. Highs will generally be higher than the Growth and Income category and lows will generally be lower. There is more risk in this category, but not the most.

The top of the pyramid is the *Aggressive Growth* risk category where you have the most risk. Here we will find smaller companies that are still trying to become big. Here is where we find international companies that are trying to compete with the big guys. Some of these companies may become the next great performers that continue to grow for decades like Microsoft, and some of them will become bankrupt. The market fluctuations in the Aggressive Growth category are strong. When the market is in favor of this category and those taking the risk, the reward is very attractive. When the market is out of favor, the downside is hurtful. You will see 20 to 30 even 40 percent up years, but you will also see 20, 30 even 40 percent down years! The market ride is dramatic in this category, and like an extreme roller coaster, it is not for the faint at heart.

Wayshak Pyramid®

In my practice, I have expanded the traditional investment pyramid into what I call the Wayshak Pyramid®. The Wayshak Pyramid® has become a foundation for my clients and I hope it becomes one for you. Let me build for you the Wayshak Pyramid®.

Take the investment pyramid and tip it over onto its side. Now, put a time line right through the middle.

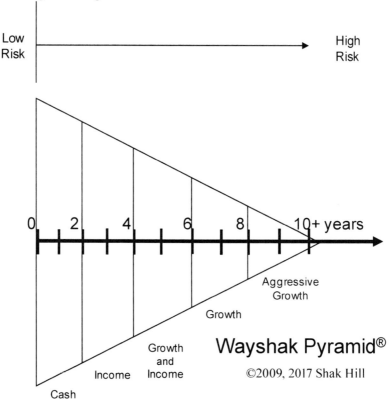

Let's walk through this illustration, starting at the left side of the pyramid.

If you need to spend money today, then you need to have the money in cash or near cash. Near cash is a money market/savings type of account or a checking account. If you are buying something today, you need to have that money immediately available. If you need to spend the money over the next two years, you still need to have it readily available. You do not have enough time to invest it.

If you don't need to spend this money for three to four years, then you can generate a little more income from it. Generally, if you invest in a three-year CD, you should get more interest than if you buy a six month CD or have it in a money market account. (This is where I put Ethel for her two-and-a-half-year CD she was using for her cruise.)

Cut Time Line in Two Parts

In the following figure, you will see that there is a squiggly curvy line that cuts the time line in two sections.

On the left of the cut are the Cash and Income risk categories. On the right are Growth and Income, Growth, and Aggressive Growth. The squiggly line is not straight because life isn't predictable. You will see the Wayshak Pyramid® is cut around the four or so year mark.

As you begin to fund your plan, you will start at the left and fill in your emergency cash and your known extras first. You have now filled in the left side of the Wayshak Pyramid®. This section represents your *Short-Term Requirements*. You *have* to have readily available money to cover emergencies, unexpected events, and normal life events. You *have* to allocate for known extras. These are important, planned events and expenditures that you predict that allow you to maintain your standard of living.

When you fill in these areas, you are filling in your short-term requirements and this should allow you to sleep very well at night, knowing that you have emergencies covered and known extras accounted for.

It is by no mistake we discussed these two questions with clients first, emergency cash and known extras. If you know the answer to

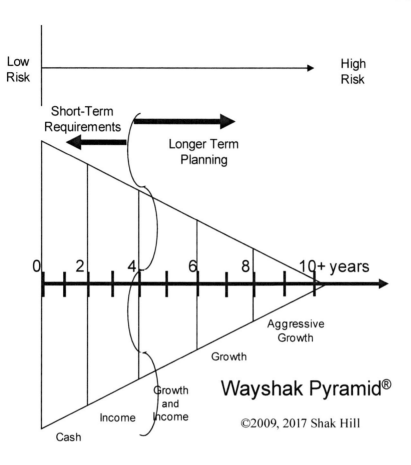

Wayshak Pyramid®

©2009, 2017 Shak Hill

these needs, then you fill up the cash needs and keep filling through the Income risk category as appropriate.

Only *after* you have filled in your short-term requirements do you have the opportunity to fill in the right portion of the pyramid, which is for longer-term planning. There is never any requirement to take Aggressive Risk. Therefore, you never have to fill to the tip of the pyramid. Perhaps you will only get as far as Growth and Income. No problem. But most experts agree you should have some of your money exposed to Growth. Now when you create your plan, you will be able to feel more comfortable that you have created it correctly.

Appropriate Risk for Time Available

A gentleman came to visit me a couple of years ago. He said that he had two years before his retirement. Because he had not saved up enough, he wanted to "go aggressive." He was looking for the "hot stock" or the "get-rich-quick" strategy. As you can see in the Wayshak Pyramid® time line, he does not have enough time to be taking that amount of risk, and I did not take him as a client.

On the other hand, my client Joann came in because her CD was maturing. After I asked her about her financial plan, she told me, "Don't worry about me, Shak, I'm diversified." I asked her to tell me more, and she shared with some degree of pride that she had this CD coming due at bank ABC and another at a different bank DEF and another CD still at another bank. I hated to be the one to tell her this, but she wasn't diversified at all.

"Joann," I explained, "You aren't diversified at all. You have all of your money in the Cash risk category. You just have different banks reporting it to you."

She had no real plans to spend this money as she had other money available for emergencies and known extras. She had time but was not taking the risk appropriate with that time—a diversified risk that will help her stay even with or outpace inflation. As it is now, at age fifty-five, she is going to start losing purchasing power after inflation and taxes, and her real rate of return probably won't keep her even with inflation.

Vast Middle

Most men populate the Wayshak Pyramid® from the top down. The Aggressive Growth category is the sexy one. This is where you buy and sell hot stocks. Here you take significant risk, which leads to wonderful bar room discussion on how much you made. When aggressive risk is being rewarded, the stories about how much money is made begin to sound like that big fish that got away or that wonderful hole-in-one golf shot. Everybody loves the up market!

When aggressive risk is not being rewarded and the market takes a downward turn, these same men get frustrated. The bar room conversation turns to women and anything but their losses. They end up selling everything, pulling their money out, and buying something else, perhaps real estate. They go from the top of the Wayshak Pyramid®, jump over the vast middle, put their money in cash, and buy something else. I start hearing, "I've lost money in the market, and I am never going to do that again." [What this usually represents is the investor who took the crazy risk of consuming the entire bottle of medicine at once. They misused the market and the medicine. They were gamblers, not planners.]

On the other hand, most women populate their Wayshak Pyramid® correctly, from the bottom up. They fill in the cash category first. Unfortunately, they continue to focus on this category. Like Joann, they just keep buying CDs or end up keeping too much in the savings, money markets, or checking accounts. Why do they do this? Because it's easy and comfortable. By not going much above the Cash or Income risk category, these same women are missing the vast middle as well.

With men, I have to push them down their Wayshak Pyramid® so they don't take too much risk. With women, I have to pull them up.

Look at the new pyramid here. You will see there is a shaded area marking the "Vast Middle." Usually within the vast middle steady, proven, long-term growth and income type of investments can easily be found, many times at reasonable prices. Investments in the vast middle can be held over a period of time, generating capital appreciation and strong income, all the while outpacing inflation and preserving your standard of living. As you create your plan, don't miss this vast middle of potentially wonderful investments.

---

*On the other hand,
most women populate
the Wayshak Pyramid®
correctly, from the
bottom up.*

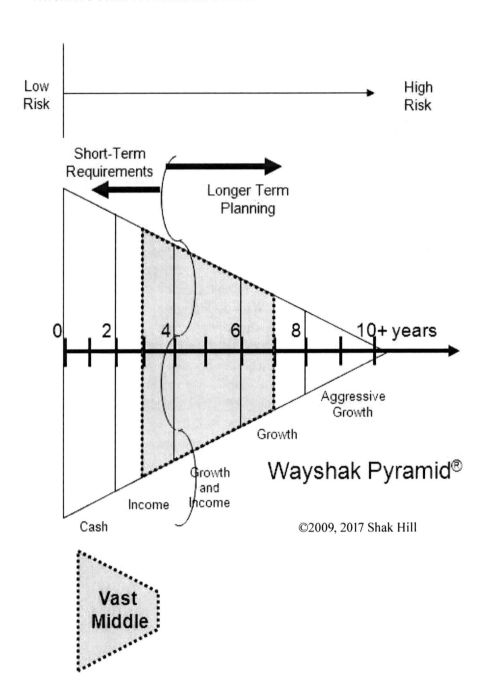

©2009, 2017 Shak Hill

KEY Concept

To summarize, investors typically take either too much risk or not enough. Although the Aggressive Growth category is available to invest in, there are investors who shouldn't be investing in the Aggressive Growth category. You can (and should) take appropriate risk based on time allowed.

The price of most goods and services go up over time. The price of a stamp will probably never come down. Allocate for your short-term requirements first, then start filling in your longer-term plan.

You cannot create a long-term plan with only short-term investments. Short-term investments are just not designed to outpace inflation or keep you ahead when you consider taxes and inflation. Work with your professional team to create a well-thought-out, comprehensive financial plan.

Omit and substitute! That's how recipes should be written.
Please don't ever get so hung up on published recipes that you
forget that you can omit and substitute.

Jeff Smith (the Frugal Gourmet)

Basic Truths about Investing

All of the ingredients you are familiar with have basic rules. Sugar is always sweet. You need to be patient as the bread rises; this cannot and should not be rushed. In fact, if you rush it, your bread will not rise. You cannot open the oven to peek at your soufflé, or it will collapse. When you marinate your meat, the sauce needs time to soak into the meat. The longer you let it marinate, the better it is. Investing in your financial future cannot be rushed either.

Another rule of ingredients is that some can be substituted. For example, regular sugar and molasses can substitute for brown sugar. There will be a flavor change, but you can still substitute. Margarine can substitute for butter, but you better have a good reason to do that. On the other hand, baking soda cannot substitute for baking powder. That would be a mess.

Investment ingredients are the same. Some ingredients cannot be rushed (darn it). Some can be substituted, yet others will not substitute at all. We need to be familiar with some of the basics of investing and some of the considerations that are needed to create your successful financial recipe.

1. Determine your **risk**.

2. Determine your **time horizon**.

3. Establish your **emergency cash needs** that lets you sleep well at night.

4. **Work with a professional and build a properly diversified portfolio** based on your personal risk tolerance. Too many clients will buy one investment here, and then get another over there, thinking they are diversified. Soon, they realize that investments bought in two different places, for the sake of diversification, are substantially the same. They are really "overlapped" in their investments; they just have two different places reporting to them. Being diversified has nothing to do with hiring several coaches to help you. You can hire one coach or financial advisor and achieve all of the diversification that you will ever need. Diversify your investments, but don't scatter.

5. **Do not delay**. You do not have the time to delay. That does not mean you should hurry or rush into an investment plan that isn't comfortable. What it does mean is that when you determine your goals and dreams, when you hire a financial advisor, when you have created your team of professionals, then build your portfolio and move forward. Many will delay and drag their feet, but this is a plan for your financial well-being. Don't put it off.

NOTE: You do not have to implement the whole plan at once. You should implement the pressing part of the plan first (perhaps a need for more income), and after you are ready, start implementing the rest.

6. **Invest to beat inflation, not the market** (unless you are willing to take on the risk of the market, which most investors are not willing to do). **Don't take too little risk**. It is easy just to buy CDs. It is easy to just do nothing. In this case, easy is often not what is right for you in the long run. You cannot do proper long-term planning with short term CDs.

7. There will always be reasons <u>not</u> to invest. **Invest anyway**.

8. Have a **reasonable expectation** of return based on the amount of risk you are taking.

9. Invest in both stocks and bonds. **Buy quality**, proven investments that have a track record of at least five years. I prefer ten years, but the lesson here is this: Don't buy something that hasn't weathered good and bad markets.

10. Where available, **reinvest**. The power of compound interest is wonderful. Stocks that pay dividends allow you to start the compounding, and with most brokerage accounts, automatic dividend reinvestment comes at no transaction charge.

11. Realize that the **market fluctuates**. By diversifying you will be in position when the market rotates to you.

12. Don't let the **tax tail wag the dog**. Taxes are part of life. We have to pay them when due. I have seen people lose money because they didn't want to pay taxes. Well, after they lost money, guess what, they still paid taxes.

13. **Don't listen to the noise**. Turn off the noise and the T.V. programs that sensationalize your emotions about the market. Remember, their

Don't get caught up in the short-term emotion and "hot stock tip" mentality.

job is to sell advertisements. So many television shows have so-called experts giving you advice. Don't forget, their sole purpose in life is to entertain and sell commercial time. Turn them off. Don't get caught up in the short-term emotion and "hot stock tip" mentality. They are not concerned about your success.

14. **Don't time the market**. No one has figured out how to time the market, so don't wait on the side and watch. Study after study shows that if an investor remains invested in good, solid, quality investments over time and they are able to ride out the short-term emotions, they end up significantly better. Consider the following chart showing how your return would have been dramatically different if you tried to time the market, but missed some of the best days.

Don't try to time the market!

If you had invested $1,000 in S&P 500
From 1/3/1995–12/31/2014

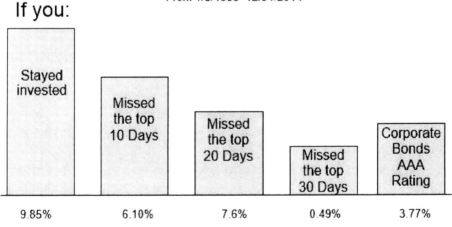

Source: J.P. Morgan, 12/31/2014

15. **Build your portfolio for the long run**. Do not focus on the gains you have made year to date. Do not look at where you are going to be in six months (that's too short). Look at how your portfolio holds up over time, in good and bad markets, and your ability to outpace inflation. Look for companies that consistently earn profits. Yes, their stock prices will ebb and flow with the economy, but should in the long run create an increasing income stream that increases your standard of living. You cannot make a long-term plan based on short-term thinking.

16. **Never buy anything you don't fully understand**. There are some complicated programs out there.

17. **Don't ever buy from someone you don't trust. Ever.**

18. **Don't chase last year's winners**. Don't chase performance. Winners can sometimes (and often) become next year's losers. Very rarely does a stock or mutual fund perform the best more than two years cause it to tank next year. Consider the following analogy:

> Think of a five-lane superhighway. You are on the superhighway, and invariably there is a slowdown and traffic has slowed to a near crawl. If you are like me, you always get into the wrong darn lane. What is the lane doing just to my left? Yep, it's moving. So what do I do? I change lanes. Now what? That lane stops, and the lane I *was* in starts moving. You know the drill. You can see it happening, and you're probably laughing at me at this very moment.

> Well, the best way to get through that slowdown is to be in all the lanes. I can't do that as I drive, but in the investment world I sure can. The best way to arrive at your financial destination is to be in all five lanes. At any given moment, you will have two or three lanes just moving right along, and if those lanes slow down or stop, then you will already be in the other lanes that start moving.

This is why you diversify. Don't jump to last year's winners just to discover they stop and the investment that you were in starts moving.

19. **Stick to Your Plan, Not to Your (and the Noisemaker's) Emotion.** Most investors buy and sell on emotion. This will most likely prove to be a mistake. Every time we turn on the news, there is another story about something. But we have to remember that two-thirds of the U.S. economy is driven by consumer spending and in the long run company stock prices will go up as they earn a profit. Short-term emotions should not prevent us from having long-term financial plans.

Wouldn't it be great if you could reach back in time and purchase such companies as AT&T, Wal-Mart, Home Depot, 3M, Johnson & Johnson, ConocoPhillips and other consistent profitable companies? If you could have purchased these and other companies ten, fifteen, even twenty years ago, think of the wealth that would have been created. It is always better to look behind and see what happened than try to look ahead and predict.

When we look behind, we see the objective reality. As we live and look ahead, we feel the emotional present and see the emotional future. The emotional present seems to somehow prevent us from making longer term plans that in the future, we will look back on and wish we had made.

Sure, not all of the decisions made would have been successful, but more would have been than not. During any time in our nation's history, there has always been bad news and otherwise reasons to be nervous about the market and the economy.

Let's consider reasons **NOT** to invest.

1941 Pearl Harbor Attacked
1950 U.S. sends troops to Korea
1957 USSR launches Sputnik
1960 Bay of Pigs
1961 Cuban Missile Crisis
1963 President Kennedy assassinated
1974 President Nixon resigns

1980 Out of control inflation
1987 President Reagan incites with "Tear down this wall"
1987 Black Monday
1991 Desert Storm
1998 President Clinton impeached
2000 Y2K
2001 9/11
2005 Hurricane Katrina
2007 Sub-prime market meltdown
2008 Record high prices for a barrel of oil and financial crisis
2009 Bernie Madoff scandal
2010 Collapse of Greece economy
2012 Benghazi attack
2014 Ferguson unrest
2015 Syria, refugees and Islamic Terrorist attacks
2016 China devalues its currency
2016 Donald J. Trump is elected president

There are always reasons not to invest. Don't let the emotions of the day prevent you from moving forward with your plan. Just think how your life would be financially different if you invested in solid blue chip companies in the early 1980s. What I would give to have been able to invest in solid companies like Coca-Cola, Wal-Mart, Johnson & Johnson, and the list goes on. Like it was mentioned in the earlier chapter, investing when there is bad news will take some courage, but courage well spent. History has shown that in spite of any reasons listed here, long-term financial wealth is created in times you least expect it.

Stock Market Clock

Economists have correctly predicted nine out of the last five recessions.
Wall Street Wit & Wisdom

The market is cyclical. It moves from top to bottom to top again. As the economy continues, the market's high will over time be *higher* than it was before, and the market low over time will also be *higher* than it was before. When the market is at the top of the cycle, investors feel great, the mood about the economy is strong, prices are high and investors buy. The market high (12:00 Noon on the clock) doesn't last forever and there will surely be a slowdown.

The market will start to decline and the stock prices will start to fall.

At the bottom (six o'clock) investors are hearing a lot of noise. Layoffs, credit crunch, corporate concerns, maybe even corporate corruption, economy slowing, more layoffs. Investments are negative, maybe for the second or third year in a row. Many investors will throw their hands up and say, "I can't keep losing money. I'm just going to buy a CD. At least I'll stop the bleeding." Many investors will sell.

There is no guarantee, but so far after *every* market low, there has been recovery and economic expansion. The economy reinvents itself and moves again. People start feeling better, but take on the attitude, "We'll just wait and see." Markets start to rise. News is not as bad (because good news is rarely reported). Okay now I'm feeling a little better. It is getting close to the top again, so I will buy. And the cycle continues.

Look at the Stock Market Clock and see if you recognize your emotional self.

We all know it is best to buy low and sell high. Because of emotion and the lack of a plan to keep us on course, we usually do the opposite. Intellectually, we know that every market downturn has led to a market upturn. Emotionally, we hear all the noise, lose heart in our investment,

get spooked by all the negative that we hear, and pull out at the market low. Build a strong plan and you will be well on your way to not making these kinds of short-sighted, emotional mistakes.

Thoughts

Courage is one of the seven essential ingredients we need to consider that will help you outpace inflation and increase your net worth. Study the Wayshak Pyramid® and the Stock Market Clock. Identify the emotional aspects and understand what they say. Even though the market is not best suited for the emotionally faint at heart, it is the best option for those who plan on living.

Remember that medicine bottle? Take the medicine like it is designed to be used, and your ailment will be cured. Mistreat it and you'll likely overdose. Investments are the same way. If you create your emergency pot and allocate for known extras, then fill in your Wayshak Pyramid® and properly diversify, overtime you will have a recipe for success and an increased likelihood of achieving your goals and dreams. But if you take investments and the market and mistreat it, trying to make a fast buck or double your money overnight, you could possibly overdose and kill yourself.

One way to help you properly use investments to fit your need is to use your professional team to support you with your decisions. In the next chapter, we will talk about doing just that and creating your professional management team.

———

But if you take investments and the market and mistreat it, trying to make a fast buck or double your money overnight, you could possibly overdose and kill yourself.

———

6

*P*rofessional Management Team

When the train goes through a tunnel and the world gets dark, do you jump out?
OF COURSE NOT!
You sit still and trust the engineer to get you through.
Corrie ten Boom

Have you heard of the culinary dish "hot dogs a la Shak"? Sure you have, well, maybe not. Hot dogs a la Shak is the best hot dog dish ever created by man! You take as many hot dogs as you fancy, cook in a frying pan, no oil, just hot dog, metal and heat. Cook to taste, cut into bite-sized pieces, place in a casserole dish, then pour your favorite baked beans over the top of the cooked hot dogs. Be creative here if you wish. You can have everyday baked beans, or you can really load them up. Add cheese topping to taste, bake at 350 degrees for ten minutes (or until cheese melts) and serve hot!

With much pride, I have shared my very own college staple that helped me through those hunger pangs. You will be further pleased to know that the recipe is now defunct, kind of like the Latin language. Once I married, hot dogs a la Shak was no more.

So why this (true) story? Because you would not come to me for cooking advice. No matter how good your doctor, dentist, seamstress, lawn maintenance man, pool boy, golf pro, roofer, or auto mechanic, no matter how fantastic they are at their particular expertise, I would wager that they don't know much about cooking. There are exceptions, but you would be best served to go to a chef if you were looking for cooking excellence.

This seems obvious, so why do so many good people take financial advice from electrical engineers, lawyers, friends, neighbors, and other well-meaning family members? The financial world is much too complicated to accept advice from people who are not experts, especially if you have a large sum of money.

Looking for the Light

You (and your husband) may never have used a professional in the past. Perhaps you filed your own taxes, did your own investments, and never really thought much about hiring someone to help. Now, it is just you, and you should give consideration to seeking professional help.

Depending on the complexity of the estate, your life has just become very complicated and certainly very uncertain. You can find great relief in hiring the right people to be on your team. As the complexity of the estate grows, so will the need to have more professionals on your team. If the estate is pretty straightforward, you may only need an attorney and financial advisor. No matter what, all professionals should be able to guide you through the process, making the "complicated" easier and helping you avoid the common mistakes that can cost you big.

Consider the following sobering thought with the IRS:

> A small mistake with a small amount of money will result in a small penalty. The exact same small mistake with a large amount of money will result in a large penalty.

The federal government doesn't care if we get 90 percent of estate planning documents correct. If it is 10 percent wrong, the whole document can be thrown out. And, unfortunately, the federal government lets us make financial mistakes. They also love it when we don't take

------

A small mistake with a small amount of money will result in a small penalty. The same exact small mistake with a large amount of money will result in a large penalty.

------

advantage of certain financial benefits available within current law. In fact, the government has set it up that our mistakes are their gain.

Making Informed Decisions

When beggars and shoe-shine boys, barbers and beauticians
can tell you how to get rich, it is time to remind yourself that there
is no more dangerous illusion
than the belief that one can get something for nothing.

Bernard Baruch

No matter how you have accumulated this money either by way of death, divorce, inheritance, or sale of assets, you need to have a firm understanding of where you are now. You should have a good understanding of your income and your assets. Now, you need to start putting the ingredients together according to *your* personal recipe, to make the most out of *your* life.

So far, we have talked about the need to speak with several different professionals. Now, let's talk about the different professionals you will come in contact with and how they fit in your plan.

Fees

Just a quick thought about fees. I discuss under each professional below how they get paid. One important thing for you to consider: when you pay a professional fee, you are paying for that person's experience and knowledge. You need to gleam valuable information from that experience. If you are not gaining from the relationship, then you are most likely overpaying.

Attorney

Most likely, one of your first appointments will need to be with an Estate Planning Attorney. Let's cover: What are estate planning attorney qualifications? What is the attorney's role? Do you need an attorney anyway? How do they get paid?

What Are Their Qualifications?

Just knowing the law isn't enough. There needs to be "real world" experience to ensure your plan works the way you want it to.

While an attorney must pass the bar to practice law, many states do not have strict requirements or formalized licensure for specialty fields like estate planning or real estate law. While many lawyers in a practice area engage in ongoing continuing legal education, it is always a good idea to do some research or get a referral.

When you need services from professionals, you look for professional accomplishments and ongoing expertise in that field. For example, if you were going to have a baby, you would look for a medical doctor who had specialized training and education in the area of obstetrics and gynecology. When looking for an attorney, assure yourself that the attorney has relevant experience, formal education and is certified in that field.

All attorneys are not educated alike. Look for a good educational background. A strong law school can be beneficial when it comes to determining the strength of that attorney. Additionally, as estate planning can be tricky enough, when it comes to taxable estates, I encourage you to consider an attorney with an LL.M. (Master in Laws) degree in taxation. The LL.M. degree is comparable to an MBA in business and management disciplines. This degree should give you additional expertise with a taxable estate - an expertise that should help identify potential taxation issues and prevent costly mistakes.

An estate planning attorney should at least do 50 percent of his or her work in the estate planning field. For more complicated cases, seek an attorney who exclusively deals with estate planning. I personally would not go to an attorney who can help me (a) sue my neighbor, (b) divorce my wife, (c) sell my home, and, oh by the way, (d) settle my estate.

Although there is no hard-and-fast rule, it takes time and experience for an attorney to fully understand the ever-changing estate laws, to know what you as the client are really looking to do, and to have the experience and ability to translate your wishes to a document that will be executed and acted upon after your death. The skilled estate planning attorney will understand the law - that is a given - but will also know which questions to ask and what pitfalls to avoid.

Just knowing the law isn't enough. There needs to be "real world" experience to ensure your plan works the way you want it to. Don't feel embarrassed to ask how many documents per month the attorney is creating, how many years has the attorney been in this field, and in what other areas of the law does the attorney practice. After all, this is your legacy that the lawyer is building within the confines of words on a piece of paper.

Many areas of law have established "board certified" distinctions. An attorney can hold himself or herself to be "board certified" in estate planning only after years of experience and demonstration of technical expertise in the field. A board certified estate planning attorney is vital for more complicated estates, and it certainly doesn't hurt for any level estate.

The American College of Trust and Estate Counsel (ACTEC) is another outstanding source when researching the credentials of your attorney. ACTEC was created to allow estate planning professionals a venue for excellence in estate planning. According to their Web site www.actec.org, the purpose of the organization is:

> "To maintain an association, international in scope, of lawyers skilled and experienced in the preparation of wills and trusts; estate planning; probate procedure and administration of trusts and estates of decedents, minors and incompetents; to improve and reform probate, trust and tax laws, procedures, and professional responsibility; to bring together qualified lawyers whose character and ability will contribute to the achievement of the purposes of the College ..."

Look into your local estate planning council. I'm the Chair of the Catoctin Estate Planning Council Education Committee in Northern Virginia and was a board member of the Brevard Estate Planning Council when I lived in Florida. These local councils have dedicated professionals who receive year-round education and professional guidance. Check to see if the attorney you are considering belongs to the local council.

Every state has a state bar association, generally located in the state capital city. Contact the bar association and ask for a directory of estate planning attorneys (that is, attorneys who have reported that they practice in estate planning). This list will be a helpful start.

What is the attorney's role? The attorney's role is to make sure you are legally protected and your wishes are clearly explained in estate documents and within the laws of the state where you live. If you are settling an estate, he or she will guide you as to the proper notices needed and when and how to close the estate. You can rely on the attorney's office to do as much or as little administration as you would like. You can do some of the running around to the probate court and to the clerk's office. Or the attorney can do that for you. Of course, you should expect the bill to be different (and more) if the lawyer's office is doing all of the work.

One widow I helped had originally turned over twenty-three of her husband's stock certificates to the attorney for processing. After she learned that I performed that service free of charge (and still do), she went back to the attorney, retrieved all twenty-three stock certificates and gave them to me. We processed them within my policy of a twenty-four hour turnaround. Again, at no charge to her.

Make sure when you meet with the attorney you ask for a written summary of the meeting, particularly if you are still working to settle the estate. If, at the time, you are in a highly emotional state, you may operate normally within the day, but, because of the tremendous stress of this new reality, a month later you may have little or no recollection of the meeting. You may want to bring a spiral notebook to take notes of your own to reference later to remind you of the material that was covered. This note taking will also serve as a helpful journal of actions taken and why they were taken, to review as needed down the road.

If you are meeting the attorney for your own planning, make sure the attorney translates all the legal jargon for you. There should be a cover page on all your estate planning documents that spells out in plain English what the documents say. The legal terminology is important to pass statutory regulation, but you may want to give strong consideration to creating your own summary document, no more than a couple of pages, that explains in your own words what your decisions are and why you have decided them.

Settling an estate is no easy task. You can lean as heavily as you want on the attorney, or as lightly.

> Nadia decided to take on as much as she could. She went everywhere, filed everything, and handled 90 percent of all the probate, notification, submission to the court, and other requirements. She used the attorney as a "tour guide" pointing out what needed to be done, and then she did it. On the other hand, Suzanne didn't want to do a thing. She used her attorney as the do-it-all for her. Neither way is correct and neither way is wrong. You decide the role.

Do you really need an attorney anyway? Because there is so much information on the internet, you can find just about anything there, including estate planning forms. If not on the Internet, there are books and computer programs that you can check out at the library that will help you create your own estate planning documents. Proceed very cautiously if you do this. In the probate process, the attorney knows exactly what to do, when to do it, and can do so much faster than you can. If the attorney makes a mistake, then he or she is professionally liable to fix it at no cost to you. If you make a mistake, the money that you thought you were going to save by doing it yourself could be spent twice over having an attorney come back behind you and clean it up.

If you are creating your own estate planning documents, remember is your legacy. If one thing is invalid in your documents, then the court could throw out the entire document. Your will might be invalidated for some innocuous reason like not being properly witnessed. If your will is thrown out, then your estate will be governed by intestacy laws (and this is the least desirable way to pass assets).

> Peter was a smart man who had a PhD and was very computer savvy. He was a do-it-yourself kind of guy who didn't want to pay for legal help. He downloaded the estate forms but never acted on them. He died suddenly of a heart attack. Nothing signed. Nothing was executed within the law. The major complication was that this was his second marriage. He had children from

both marriages, and there was no direction about his estate. The legacy he left was not the one he had intended.

How do attorneys get paid? Many attorneys charge a flat fee to create the documents you need. After the initial consultation (which is usually free), they should let you know what documents you need and what the fee will be. Some will charge by the hour, so make sure that you get a strong estimate as to how many hours it will take.

In the selection process, be mindful of expenses but don't make your decision based solely on them. Depending on your situation, you may need someone with greater skill and knowledge. This attorney may be more expensive. That is to be expected. If you get someone who specializes in estate planning, he or she will most likely spend less time having to "learn" what to do than someone else who will do it for you and charge less per hour, yet take more hours.

Life Insurance Agent

The second most important person to see after your husband's death is your life insurance professional.

The best place to start is to find the agent who sold the policy in the first place. If you are unable to locate that person or if they have already retired, then find someone in the field to help you.

Be aware of a couple of things. First, if you are able to use the insurance professional who sold the policy, he or she will be able to walk you through the different settlement options. Because the agent was compensated at the time of the sale, this service at your husband's passing should be at no charge to you. Second, if you use another insurance professional other than the one who sold your husband the policy, you will need to determine what the charges for service will be. This agent has not been compensated for the sale of the policy, so he or she will most likely charge a fee.

Because the agent was compensated at the time of the sale, this service at your husband's passing should be at no charge to you.

If there is more than one policy, you need to contact each agent or company of your husband's passing and request death claim kits. This kit will have directions as to how to file a claim for the proceeds and what documents they require to pay the claim. They will each ask you for (but are not limited to) the following:

- A death certificate.
- The original policy or a statement from you of a "lost" policy, if it cannot be located.
- Letter of instruction if you are the beneficiary, or the Letters of Testamentary you received from the probate court if you are not the beneficiary.
- Details as to how you are requesting the benefits, whether lump sum or payout over time.

As you look for a life insurance professional, be aware of the same questions you investigated about attorneys.

What are their qualifications? Life Insurance agents are licensed. Each state has a Department of Insurance, Insurance Commissioner, or some area that is designated just to monitor insurance sold within the state. The insurance agent needs to be licensed by the state in order to conduct insurance business with citizens of that state. The agent will have taken insurance tests and is required to obtain continuing educational hours to remain in compliance with state laws. Generally, these CE (Continuing Education) hours deal with industry rules, latest innovations available, and ethical and behavior standards. This is the minimum for being able to transact insurance business.

Insurance professionals that show strong dedication to the field will seek to achieve one or both of the following professional designations.

- **Chartered Life Underwriter** (CLU®): The American College (www.theamericancollege.edu) confers this professional designation. The CLU has been around since 1927 helping families and businesses with extensive insurance planning. The professional obtaining the CLU is highly educated with a rigorous educational program, has required experience in the field, and can provide a wide range of financial planning and insurance expertise. There are continuing educational requirements that have to be met as well as professional standards of conduct combined with ethical training.

- **Chartered Financial Consultant** (ChFC®): As the financial world became more complicated, the ChFC was created in 1982 to further enhance the insurance professional. As important as the CLU is, the ChFC takes the next step by including financial planning and wealth creation. The American College (www. theamericancollege.edu) confers this professional designation. The ChFC also has strict continuing educational requirements that have to be met as well as professional standards of conduct combined with ethical training.

What is the insurance agent's role? If you are settling your husband's estate, the insurance agent will help you file the claim and guide you to the type of payout that is best for your situation.

Lump sum: In the days of old, the insurance company would normally mail you a death benefit check for the amount owed. You would then take that check to the bank and deposit it there. Nowadays, the insurance companies are themselves hoping to be your "bank" and seek to hold the money on your behalf. If you have selected the lump sum option, they will send you a checkbook representing the full amount of the benefit. You are under no obligation to keep the money there with them, and you can write a single check, close out their account and deposit the check into your bank. If you choose to leave the money with the insurance company, make certain that you are receiving a competitive interest rate.

The longer you "require" the insurance company to pay out, the lower the payment will be.

Periodic payments: You can turn the death benefit into an income stream for a period of time that you designate. This period can be determined by a fixed number of years, say twenty years, or it can be for the rest of your life (which could either be long or short, hopefully long!). Keep this concept in mind: The longer you "require" the insurance company to pay out, the lower the payment will be. If the company is not required to pay out, then the payment will be the highest. These payments are based on your current age and life expectancy. Let me give you an example (for illustration purposes only):

> Let's say you are receiving a death benefit of a certain amount, and you are sixty years old. If you take this benefit for life, you might receive $700 month. If you require the insurance company to pay someone for at least ten years, whether you are alive or not, then you would elect the "Life plus 10 Years Certain" option and perhaps receive $650 a month. If you want to guarantee someone gets paid for twenty years, you would elect the "Life plus 20 Years Certain" and perhaps receive $500 a month.

In this illustration, you receive the most payment if you take it for your life only. Using the "Law of Large Numbers" concept, some taking this option will live long, some will live for a predictable time, and some will live short. If you require the insurance company to pay for a period of time, then your payment will decrease.

Do you really need an agent anyway? The CLU and the ChFC professional will help you make an informed decision that best meets your needs. One last important note, once you have made your election, it cannot be undone. I strongly recommend you seek and pay for advice, if warranted, so you fully understand the choices you have.

How do they get paid? The best part of having the life insurance professional helping you right now is that there should be little cost to you. The commission was paid when the policy was issued. There should be little or no cost for wisdom now that the policy is being collected. You should not feel guilty about not paying the agent. He or she was paid, and this is part of the service. If the professional you are working with did not sell the original policy, you may want to double check about the expectancy of payment. Again, most professionals will not charge a fee, even if they didn't sell the policy in the first place.

Financial Advisor

This is a little tricky so I need you to stay with me regarding the explanation of a financial advisor.

This is a little tricky so I need you to stay with me regarding the explanation of a financial advisor. There are generally two different levels of advice available in the market place. The "broker" or "registered representative" works for a broker dealer (the company that they are affiliated with) and provides to you "suitable" recommendations for products that are designed to meet your financial needs. On the other hand, "Investment Advisor Representative" (IAR) provides "fiduciary" advice and has a higher standard to match your overall needs with solutions in your best interest.

You will want to know if your adviser is a broker or an IAR.

What are their qualifications? You will be surprised to know that there are *very few* formal qualifications in order to be called a financial advisor. This is one area of the financial industry that is not heavily regulated, and there are little guidelines as to *what* makes someone a "financial advisor."

You will be surprised to know that there are very few *formal qualifications in order to be called a financial advisor.*

As you know, clearly defined requirements exist for doctors and lawyers. You have to be admitted to practice medicine and law and those admitting agencies require significant education and practical background. The financial world has a governing body called FINRA. This stands for Financial Industry Regulatory Authority. FINRA does regulate the industry, overseeing brokerage firms and registered representatives. But with this oversight, *you* have to do your homework, because not all financial advisors are the same.

A financial advisor has to pass certain tests and maintain minimum continuing educational standards. The similarity ends here. There are vast differences between the education, background, experience, and other qualifications of financial advisors.

NOTE: You may want to review FINRA's web site, www.finra.org. It is there for your use!

What are some characteristics of a broker? After passing entrance exams and maintaining continuing educational requirements, there are no formal additional requirements. When you are looking for an advisor, make sure to ask, "What makes you a financial advisor?" You should look for the following:

Series 6 *Investment Company and Variable Contracts Products Representative*
Series 7 *General Securities Representative* (preferred over the Series 6)
Life Insurance
Variable Life and Annuity License
Health Insurance

A broker helps you transact business and gets paid a commission for this service.

What are some characteristics of an Investment Advisor Representative (IAR)? The IAR also needs to pass entrance exams and maintain continuing educational requirements. At certain levels of business management, the IAR will need to register with the state and then with the federal government. This person does not act as a broker and can not charge a commission. Instead, the IAR will charge a fee for advice, discussed a little later in this chapter.

What else can you look for?

After verifying what type of advisor you are working with, you will want to ask if they have any of the following:

Academic accomplishments:
Undergraduate degree (Finance-related field preferred)
Graduate degree (Finance-related field preferred)

Professional designations within the industry:
CERTIFIED FINANCIAL PLANNER, CFP® (discussed in detail later)
Chartered Life Underwriter, CLU® (discussed previously)
Chartered Financial Consultant, ChFC® (discussed previously)
Certified Public Accountant, CPA
Chartered Financial Analyst, CFA
The Chartered Institute of Management Accountants, CIMA

CAUTION: There has been an enormous growth of "designations" available. Be aware that anyone can *create* a designation, so please be careful to research the particular designations that you see. There are many out there, but only a few are well respected and represent industry excellence, and those are listed here.

NOTE: Some states are beginning to weigh in on the designations they will allow to be used by professionals in that state. For example, Nebraska and Massachusetts have legislated certain designations may not be used in their states.

What is the financial advisor's role? In my opinion, when you look for help with finances, you should look for someone who is going to take a holistic approach to your financial situation. This person should review your overall status, first looking at your goals. He or she should help you identify what your goals are and the amount of risk you are willing to take in order to accomplish those goals. The advisor will need to know about your income, debts, insurances, and investments. Next, he or she should then help you to construct a diversified portfolio and complement your planning with insurance protection and any other planning you require. He or she should make recommendations as to the solutions in the marketplace that will help you with your goal and will stay with you as you implement those recommendations.

When you hire your advisor, you should look at this person as your coach, quarterback, and coordinator.

When you hire your advisor, you should look at this person as your coach, quarterback, and coordinator. I often tell clients that I am like a wedding planner. I don't bake the cake, but I figure out which one is best for you. Or, think of a doctor. The doctor doesn't make the penicillin, but knows when to give you a shot, where to give it to you and what to do if there is an allergic reaction. I don't make the investments, but, after learning what your goals are, I figure out which one meets your every criterion, and that's the one we get. If there is an 'allergic reaction' and the investment doesn't work out, then we get a different one.

> *This recipe is certainly silly. It says to separate the eggs,*
> *but it doesn't say how far to separate them.*
> Gracie Allen

Do you really need a financial advisor anyway? Here's where we see the difference between advice and wisdom. Occasionally I get the question, "Why do people pay you for advice? I can get it by watching the TV or by calling into some talks show on the radio for free." My answer is always the same, "*Their* job is to sell commercials and advertising space. *My* job is to work directly with you and your financial goals. They don't know anything about you, where you are from, or where you want to go."

In reality, everybody can give you advice: magazine writers, your next-door neighbor and your son-in-law can give you advice. Recognize that some members of the family and even friends may try to help you with finances. Some will try to give you the "hot stock of the day" pick to help you grow your money. Others will offer you "business" opportunities, if only you invest a small amount of money with them for some ground-breaking opportunity. Resist both.

Also resist the new stranger in your life that looks at you as a lonely woman with a new inheritance and is looking to remove you of the same. It is sad but true; they are out there. What is sometimes even sadder is they may appear even within your family. Everybody will give you advice. I would argue that you are not looking for advice, you are looking for wisdom.

Webster's dictionary tells us *wisdom* means "knowledge, insight, judgment," and *advice* means "recommendation regarding a decision or course of conduct."

Anyone can recommend, only certain professionals can give you knowledge, insight, and judgment. When you confide in a financial advisor, you should demand wisdom, not advice.

In the world today there is so much information out there and so many opinions that it is very difficult to know what applies to you, or if you are an exception. From twenty-four-hour news sources to "Your Money" segments on every news broadcast to CNBC displaying the time to the hundredths of a second, you can find information and advice everywhere you turn. But it is only when that information is interpreted to your specific needs, coupled with formal education, excellence, and integrity, that wisdom comes out to support you, serve you, and make certain that you are accomplishing what *you* want to, not what *they* want to sell you.

I heard a joke not too long ago that brings home the point.

> A granddaughter asked her grandmother, "How old are you?" The grandmother answered with a smile, "I don't give my age out and I am not going to start by telling you." Well the granddaughter put her shoulders back and down. Pumped out her chest a bit and said with a little pride, "Grandmother, I know how old you are. You see, I was just in your bedroom, and I noticed on your bureau that you had your purse. Inside your purse I found your driver's license. Your license told me a lot about you. It tells me the color of your hair, the color of your eyes, how tall you are, and even how much you weigh. And, if I take your birthday and subtract it from today, well I know that you are seventy-three years old."

> The grandmother answered, "Well, that is quite true."

> The granddaughter just shook her head side-to-side and said, "But grandmother, I was so disappointed to learn that you received an *F* in sex."

Anyone can recommend, only certain professionals can give you knowledge, insight, and judgment.

This is a great example of information with no wisdom. There is a difference and you deserve wisdom.

How do financial advisors provide service? As it is with anything, you have to pay for good service, and the financial advisor is no different. One of the most frequent complaints I hear from investors regarding our industry is, "My investment advisor never calls me unless he is trying to sell me something." This is true. The broker's job is to help you with ideas and investment advice, but the broker doesn't get paid unless you buy or sell something.

Different levels of service are available and generally they fall into one of three service categories. The best way to illustrate this is the example of getting the oil changed in your car. Generally, there are only three different ways you can change the oil:

1. You can do it yourself. This is the cheapest way, but you have to know how to do all of the work, do it correctly and you have to properly dispose of the oil.
2. You can go to a discount location and hope the attendant had proper training. You also have to hope he actually does what he says he is going to do and what you paid him to do.
3. You can go back to the dealership where you get an ASE certified mechanic and the backing of the dealership. If you have a service plan with them, they will call you to remind you to get the oil changed. They may even pick up your car and drop it back off.

Which one of these methods is going to give you the best service?

Which one will be working with you about your overall performance of your vehicle? Which one cares most about your business? Which one knows your name?

I equate these three ways to change your oil to the service you are going to find from financial advisors.

1. You can do it yourself. Go online and make all of the decisions. This is the cheapest way.

2. You can use a discount brokerage, and they will help you get into the market. Many times they will not give you advice or wisdom about your situation. They will just direct you to their web site and the tools and calculators available there. The same tools and calculators I have on my web site, www. YourFinancialGuidingLight.com.

3. You can use a full-service financial advisor. This person knows you and your goals. In many cases, they will be able to give specific advice and wisdom based on your unique needs. You will pay an annual fee or fee of some kind.

Which one of these professionals is going to give you the best service? Which one will be working with you about your overall performance of your financial plan? Which one has a personal stake in your success? Which one knows you by name?

NOTE: There are a lot of people who change their own oil and go to discount oil companies. You will want to determine which level of service and expertise you are looking for as you decide whom to hire for your team.

How they get paid? There are many ways that financial advisors get paid for services. Generally there are three ways: hourly charge, plan charge, and fee-based charge.

- **Hourly charge**: The financial advisor who charges hourly is doing just that. Be certain to know how much they charge per hour and approximately how many hours your case should take. If the planner has strong industry experience, he or she should be able to give you an accurate estimate as to the total expense you should be incurring. Make certain you understand this going in, and what the policy is if the hours are exceeded. This financial advisor will provide you with a plan based on your existing assets, your goals, and your time horizon. You are then free to go to others and implement your plan.

- **Plan charge**: Some financial advisors charge a flat rate for a plan. During the intake, the planner will get all of your personal data. Once he or she has all the data, the planner will know if your financial status is straightforward or if it is more complicated. If your finances are complicated, the charge will understandably be greater than if your finances are more straightforward. When the plan is completed, the planner will walk you through the findings. At this point you are free to go to others to implement the recommendations. Sometimes, this type of planner will offer to implement the recommendations. They may even reduce the overall price of the plan if they implement some or the entire plan.

- **Fee based**: Some financial advisors will offer the written plan as a courtesy with the expectation of implementing the entire plan when the process is completed. This planner will charge a fee based on the amount of money invested and managed according to your plan. Under this pricing arrangement, there will be ongoing communication and update of the plan at no additional expense to you. You would continue to employ this planner as long as there were services rendered and value added. Many clients like this approach because not only do they get a strong plan but they can implement that plan with the same person and won't have to explain everything all over again.

There is no right or wrong way to go when hiring a planner. Find someone with strong credentials, experience, and a burning desire to help you accomplish your goals.

Find someone with strong credentials, experience, and a burning desire to help you accomplish your goals.

Professional Designations

There are many designations in this industry and more popping up. Here is a discussion on the most widely known and respected ones.

CERTIFIED FINANCIAL PLANNER™

Probably the best known and most recognizable designation in the financial planning arena is the CERTIFIED FINANCIAL PLANNER™, the CFP®. The CFP® designation was created in 1986 to set basic standards by what is now known as the Certified Financial Planner Board of Standards, Inc. (CFP® Board). Their web site is www.cfp.net. This Board oversees the CFP® process ensuring educational standards, work experience, and ethical standards are met. The Board has disciplinary action available for practitioners who no longer meet or by action have no longer earned the ability to call themselves CFP® practitioners.

To earn the CFP® designation, the candidate must pass comprehensive educational classes in:

- General Principles in Financial Planning
- Insurance Planning and Risk Management
- Employee Benefits Planning
- Estate Planning
- Investment Planning
- Income Tax
- Retirement Planning

After completing these prerequisites, the candidate must then pass a comprehensive two-day test covering these topics and applying them to several case studies. The overall pass rate on this test is 63 percent[1]. Additionally, the candidate must show evidence of hands-on work in the field for a period of years.

In order to maintain status as a CFP® professional, a planner needs to accomplish continuing education, ethical training, and agree to abide by a professional code of ethics, pledging to conduct business with integrity and objectivity and in the best interest of the client.

[1] http://www.cfp.net

Chartered Financial Analyst

The Chartered Financial Analyst (CFA) emphasizes security analysis and overall portfolio construction. A CFA probes the detail of companies and works on creating investment portfolios. The CFA concentrates on analysis of individual stocks and the products that are available to the general public. In order to achieve this designation, the candidate must pass three major exams as well as have three years of analytical experience. According to the www.CFAInstitute.org the pass rate for those who get to Level III is 53%. Additionally, there are continuing education requirements as well as a pledge to conduct business ethically.

Certified Public Accountant

The Certified Public Accountant (CPA) is the designation that is achieved when the candidate passes the Uniform CPA Examination. This exam is given after evidence of an undergraduate degree in accounting or other related field. Additionally, there are continuing education requirements as well as a pledge to conduct business ethically.

CLU and ChFC

These important designations have been discussed earlier in this chapter.

There are other professionals that you may come in contact with.

Registered Representative (you might call them a stockbroker)

Most investors still work with the traditional registered representatives or stockbrokers. This professional generally works for a commission paid when a product is bought or sold. If you are receiving more services from your stockbroker, then you will generally pay a "full service" fee. If you are receiving fewer services, then you will pay more of a retail or a la carte fee. Some stockbrokers are moving toward financial planning, but many still operate on commission.

The requirements to become a stockbroker are few. You must pass the Series 7 exam, which is administered through FINRA. That's about it. There is no requirement for higher education. There are continuing education requirements that need to be accomplished annually.

Banker

You will need to use the services of the local banker. When you walk into the branch, work with the customer service representative. All banks have them, but they are usually called something different depending on the bank. Some are Financial Specialists, Customer Service Representatives, or Financial Service Representatives, or something like that. They are excellent sources to help you open the estate account, transfer joint accounts to single accounts, and conduct other traditional banking services. Many banks are requiring that their bankers become licensed to sell products to you. There is nothing wrong with this, but if you have a financial advisor, make sure that you coordinate with him or her before you buy something from the bank.

Trust Banker

Most, if not all banks, have trust departments. This fiduciary department will manage money for you and provide other personal services. Your husband may have named a bank as successor trustee. You will have a trust officer assigned to you regarding this appointment. The trust departments offer a wide range of services that may be beneficial to you. Make sure that you recognize that your husband's naming of them is a nomination that has to be confirmed with the court. If for some reason there is conflict or tension, you may seek relief from the court or even ask the bank to resign as successor trustee.

Making Your Selection

Once you have decided upon the level of service you are looking for and the expertise you will need, then it is time to interview and narrow down your selection. I would call at least two professionals in each area of need and let them know that you are looking for help. They will usually meet with you as a courtesy to see if there is a good fit. You may feel comfortable bringing a family member with you or a friend. They are expecting this. Ask the following questions:

o What is your education level?

o What are your professional designations?

o Who is your ideal client?

o Do you work with clients in my situation?

o What is the total assets that you have under management? What is the total number of clients that you have? What is the largest amount that you manage?

o What is the amount of assets that you manage for your average client? You don't want to be the highest where he or she is learning from your account, and you don't want to be the lowest where you are lost among higher level accounts.

o How do you get paid? There is no shame in asking this question. You will need to pay for services rendered, but you don't need to *overpay* for them.

o How long has your longest client been with you?

o Who are your team members? Will I be dealing with you or with one of them? Often there is a "rainmaker" in an office, but, once a client, you may get assigned to someone else. Nothing necessarily wrong with that but you will want to know if this is the case going in.

o Ask for references. When you get them, call them.

o You may wish to work with someone who is younger than you. This person will most likely be able to support you for the rest of your life.

Make sure there is chemistry between the two of you. Did you feel comfortable? Did the explanations go over your head or were they at your level of understanding?

What is the recipe for successful achievement?
To my mind there are just four essential ingredients: Choose
a career you love, give it the best there is in you, seize your
opportunities, and be a member of the team.

Benjamin F. Fairless

If you were going to have a pot luck dinner party at your home, you would at least want to make sure everybody had something different to bring. Without coordination, you could have all desserts (although that might not be bad) or all appetizers. To avoid this you would probably assign a type of dish by the person's last name, or everyone on this street brings meat, this other street salad.

As you start hiring professionals to support you, make sure that they know about the others you are hiring.

Your financial plan needs to be equally coordinated. Now that you have your team, you need to make sure that their individual efforts are collectively going to work as planned for you.

Introduce Each to the Other

As you start hiring professionals to support you, make sure that they know about the others you are hiring. Your lawyer, financial advisor, CPA, and insurance agent should be aware of the others. You may even feel comfortable having them coordinate with each other about your planning. In today's financial world, finances are more complicated than just one person or one discipline.

> Diane always copies her attorney Roger on the decisions I make with her. I have brought up issues Diane confirms with Roger, and the three of us send e-mails back and forth supporting Diane and her financial goals. We each know what the other is advising and how each piece fits in with her goals. It is a great win-win-win for Diane.

Life Boat Drill

I heard it referred to as a "life boat drill" at one of my continuing education conferences. What is this, you ask? Well, if you have ever been on a cruise, one of the very first things you do is a life boat drill in case of a disaster at sea. You have to put on one of those silly bright orange life vests and then work your way on deck and stand under your assigned life boat. This serves several purposes. One, it gets you to recognize you have an assigned boat. Two, it shows you where that boat is. Three, you get to see how ridiculous all of your boat-mates look in bright orange life vests.

Financially, you should have a life boat drill as well. This is when you get all your professional team together in one room. You simulate a crisis, and you discover what each of them is going to do for you. Who is going to contact family? Who is going to coordinate immediate care? How is the trust going to work? Who should the successor trustee and executor call first? Make sure you ask about all the other important issues that are unique to your personal situation.

Don't Buy That; Blame It on Me

When you have your team together, you will most likely see your financial advisor the most. You have created your legal documents, so if there is no change there, you probably won't see the attorney much. Same with your insurance professional and the CPA. But you should see the financial advisor regularly. Perhaps you are paying your planner an annual fee, so this does entitle you to reasonable contact.

My clients call me for all of their major purchases. Whether it is a car (which I know little about) or an addition on their house, or whatever, they call me up to bounce the idea off me. This is perfectly fine with me and I even expect it. A major purchase can hurt the plan, so I believe that it is important for me to know about it and even weigh in on the decision.

> Karen called and told me she was looking to buy a golf cart. I asked her if at seventy-three she was going to take up golf. No, she said. Now, I was puzzled. I have been to her house and it is not big enough for a golf cart, so why was she thinking about buying one. Karen told me that her neighbor had one and asked her to buy one. Turns out that the neighbor owned the golf cart shop! Now I see the connection. I told her that I needed to review her finances and would get back to her the next day. I also knew Karen well enough that she really didn't need or want that golf cart. Of all of the goals and dreams she had shared with me, not once did she ever mention a cart. I called her back and told her "no."

Two weeks later, she called me happy as a lark! She was able to tell the neighbor that she wanted to buy that cart, but her advisor told her no. She blamed it on me. And that is perfectly fine with me.

Fund the Estate Plan

Now that you have your team together, work with them to fund the estate plan that you and your husband created or, now if he has passed, the plan that the documents direct. Many times at the creation of the estate plan and again at the first death of either the husband or the wife, your assets will have to be re-titled in appropriate accounts. Money often times needs to be divided into several accounts per the instructions in the trust. Make sure you work with your professionals to help you with this.

Most likely, you will be working with your financial advisor to help you with this part of the plan. The best financial advisors will coordinate with your attorney, insurance agent, and accountant to implement their recommendations in your plan.

The best way to illustrate this step is to walk you through an actual case.

Robyn and Bob were married for twenty-five years when Bob passed away in 2000. Both had been married before and both of their spouses had passed away, leaving them each with two children. When they married at age forty-seven and forty-five, they knew that they would not have children together, but they wanted to care for each other while alive and leave their part of the estate to their respective children. In 1995, Bob and Robyn established trusts and instructions of what should happen when the first of them passed away. In 2000, Bob passed away.

I met Robyn in 2005, and all of the assets were in her single name. Nothing was titled into the trust. To that point in her life, Robyn had not funded the plan that they had worked on together and that the professionals had set up for them.

The concept of "funding" the estate seems to be missed by many. So I have come up with a simple, yet powerful analogy. I tell my clients that the lawyer builds the house (the trust) and it is my job as the financial advisor to move in the furniture (fund the trust). If the furniture in not in the house, it will not be within the control of the house. Therefore, if the money is not titled into the trust, it will not be within the control of the trust document.

Because Robyn had not followed the plan and all the assets remained titled in her single name, her estate would have passed via the will and probate. Even though she had a well-thought-out plan with top-quality trust documents, because everything she owned was in her single name, those trust documents would have been useless. Her will directed all her assets be split evenly between her two children. As the combined estate is worth $3 million, her two children would inherit everything, leaving Bob's children with nothing. Most likely, Bob's children would file suit against her children for their part of their father's estate.

Robyn showed me the estate documents. They directed at the first one's death, three trusts should be created. The estate would be valued and divided in half. Because Bob passed first, the first trust was to receive the exclusion amount allowable based on the year of his death, which was then $650,000. The second trust received the rest of his half of the estate. Robyn was directed to place her entire half of the estate into the third trust.

By actually funding the estate plan (moving in the furniture) the way they had directed, we were able to create an income from both of his trusts to Robyn as was directed, and prevent that lawsuit that was sure to come.

Because Robyn had not followed the plan, her estate would have passed via the will and probate.

Robyn has moved to Florida where she needs to establish domicile. I also advised her to restate her legal documents as "legal resident of the State of Florida." Quite a mess averted. And well worth the normal fees she paid for my services.

Thoughts

Whatever the estate documents say – creation of testamentary trusts, direction of gifts, and other distributions of assets, for example – make certain you fulfill those requirements. For a variety of reasons, you should work with your professional team to help you determine where you are, where you are going, and what the best way to get there is.

Your professional team will be able to guide you and add wisdom to your plan, helping you achieve your goals and dreams. Make sure that you hire the coach that fits with your personality and helps you understand the often tricky financial world. Do you need a professional team? I often save my clients more money than I could possibly bill them by not allowing them to make financial mistakes. Your team should do the same.

7

Estate Documents You Must Have

The failure or incomplete success of a recipe often times depends upon some little detail that has been misunderstood or overlooked in the preparation.
A Book for a Cook, The Pillsbury Co. (1905)

Part of every financial recipe should include how the ingredients are going to transition to those you leave behind. You should establish a goal that you will make your transition as easy as possible for your heirs. There is nothing more comforting when I speak with heirs when they say all was in order.

As we start your planning, one thing I want you to keep in mind is your legacy to your family and friends. This is your last statement to them. They will remember how the assets transferred.

Let's resolve to get it right.

Overview of Why You Should Do Estate Planning

A number of reasons exist as to why estate planning is so necessary. The following discussion is about *something that will happen*. Darn it. There is nothing we can do about it. The transition of your assets will occur. Ownership, management, and control will pass to someone else. These transitions can pose many problems, from legal, tax and other regulations, to family harmony. When creating your estate plan, you have to prepare for what might happen. Let's say there are 100 possible things that could happen at your death. [I have made up this number, so go along with me.] Out of the 100 possible things that could happen, 86 of them won't happen at all. Problem is neither you nor I know which of the fourteen *will* occur in your situation.

By establishing your documents, *you*, and not some probate bureaucrat, will decide. You decide where and to whom the assets go. You decide if a charity, church or other entity receives the money.

You decide who is to be the guardian for your minor children and how to care for your special needs adult child.

You decide to avoid probate or not.

> *You decide if a charity, church or other entity receives the money, not a judge.*

You decide that when you die you pass more than money; you pass family harmony and life lessons.

You decide what legacy you are going to leave.

You decide the last statement you are going to say when you pass away. And, of the 100 things that could happen, you decide the ones that do happen!

Through your documents, you get to say, "I love you." Creating estate documents is one of the favors we can give our family.

Gloria Lenhart learned the hard way how to navigate the world of widowhood when her husband passed away with no notice.

Among other great thoughts, in her book, *Planet Widow*, Lenhart discusses six ways to say, "I love you."

1. Sign an Advance Health Care Directive.
2. Make a list of your assets.
3. Consolidate your accounts.
4. Keep beneficiary forms up to date.
5. Review your life insurance coverage.
6. Update your will and/or trust.

The 3 Essential Estate Planning Documents

Estate planning documents allow you to: 1) decide who is going to be your decision maker, 2) give that person the power and authority to decide on your behalf and 3) give them instructions as to your wishes. It is vital you have your estate planning documents in order. Almost everyone should have these three documents:

1. Last Will and Testament
2. Health Care Directive, Advance Directive, Living Will
3. Durable Power of Attorney

(and only if needed, you should have a Trust, discussed in Chapter 13)

Last Will and Testament

Your last will and testament are your last words to your family, friends, and heirs. The will is a legal document that outlines your intentions on how to settle your estate and pass your assets to those who survive. The will has no authority while you are alive and becomes legally unchangeable at your death. The will mechanically passes your assets, but your "legacy" will be alive long after the estate is divided.

In the will, you direct assets to family, children, grandchildren, and others. You may include a friend or those who have touched you in some meaningful way. You may even specifically eliminate someone from your estate. Long after these directions are followed and completed, the legacy of your will (and estate) will live on.

Personal Representative or Executor

You have the ability to nominate your Personal Representative, Executor, or Executrix to settle your estate. Whether they are called *personal representative* or *executor* will depend on the state you live in, but their function and responsibility are the same.

You will need to give consideration as to whom you nominate. If your husband has died, you may have been appointed his personal representative and you have discovered that settling the estate is no easy task. Hopefully there was planning beforehand making his estate easy to transfer. Even with good planning, it takes time and energy to settle the estate properly. If he is alive, you will likely nominate your husband to be your personal representative, and if you don't have a husband, generally the oldest child is nominated. You will want to consider if this child is the best suited one? Sometimes the best suited is the one who lives closest to you or has a business sense on how to settle financial matters. Maybe your personal representative shouldn't be a relative at all.

It is more important to choose your personal representative based on this person's character and values, than on "blood." When it comes to settling estates, there are so many gray areas. So much so that your personal representative can make decisions completely *against* your wishes but are well within the law and the guidelines set forth in your will.

Here is an example of such a situation within the law, but certainly not what was intended.

> Mom had two boys, George and Pete. I never met the mom. I did meet George. Mom's estate was worth about $900,000, including the home and a stock portfolio of $400,000. George was the oldest son, he was named executor. The will was the traditional kind and, as their dad had already died, it said each son was to receive half. Nothing fancy, pretty straightforward.

> Through the normal delays that come with probate, the time to divide the property came about a year after the mom had passed. George and I worked up the date of death value on the stocks. He said he would get back to me as to which ones went to Pete and which ones he would keep.

> I thought this was odd. Normally, I have seen that if there were ten stocks, the number of *shares* would be divided by two and each would receive those ten stocks with half of the shares each. This certainly would be what his mom wished when she said split everything 50/50. This is not what George did.

> He knew the value of her portfolio at the date of her death was about $400,000. He tracked the progress one year later. He gave Pete all of the *underperforming* stocks and kept the better performing ones for himself. One year later, the value of the portfolio was about $440,000. Pete received about $180,000

because his share had actually lost money from the time of his mother's death, and George received $260,000 because his share had performed better.

He determined the value 50/50 using the date of death value, not the value at the time of the transfer.

You will have to weigh delicate balance when nominating your personal representative. You want someone who is familiar with the family, but perhaps not part of the family. You also want someone who is completely objective, but won't operate independently without considering family wishes. Family dynamics are important in settling issues that arise after your death, and being able to blame no - win situations on a non–family member may have strong merit in keeping family harmony long after the settling of your estate.

Laura had three daughters who were close to each other and to her. When Laura passed away, she had named her oldest daughter as her personal representative. Everything was going along well with the estate settlement until it came to a certain piece of artwork in her mother's bedroom. The painting that hung on the wall became a significant flash point with two of the daughters, the oldest and the youngest. Each had very valid reasons to want the painting, and each set her heart on getting it. The painting had some monetary value, but the driver was the emotional value.

The oldest daughter reshuffled some of the other assets to her youngest sister to make "even" in dollars the inheritance because of the value of the painting. But price wasn't the issue.

Unfortunately, you can see what happened. The oldest sister, given the authority under the will, kept the painting and displays it proudly in her home. The youngest sister refused to set foot in the home and missed important family celebrations for a couple of years.

Now the youngest sister does go, but whenever she sees the painting, there is a tear within her that is painful. Yes there was an offer to share the painting between them, but, according to the younger sister, "It was made too late and made without true intention."

> *The decisions of your personal representative will have a "legacy" effect that becomes attached to you.*

This seemingly simple decision turned into a potential destroyer of the sisters' relationship and family harmony. The decisions of your personal representative will have a "legacy" effect that becomes attached to you. If there was a separate, non–family member settling the estate, then Laura's daughters would understand that the painting can't be ripped in half and that only one of them could actually inherit it. And they would have someone other than the oldest sister to blame.

Minor Children

If you have minor children, you have to have a will. It is in this document that you name a guardian for them. One of the hardest decisions that you make is the choice of who is going to be guardian for your minor children if something should happen to you.

How do you consider one side of the family over the other? Sometimes the choice is clear, but many times it is not. Do you name the one who had no children, or the one who already has a couple? Do you name the one who is the most successful, or the one that struggles a little to get by?

My wife and I have discussed this for our children and have named one of my brothers as guardian. This decision is not the clearest or easiest. There is no clear relative who is better than another. But for the sake of the children, we still need to name someone.

In our will, we have given him the ability to make capital improvements on his current home to accommodate our six children. Certainly, he will need to add a couple of bedrooms and bathrooms to care for their basic needs. He is going to use part of their inheritance to do this. There are other provisions we have spelled out so if something happens to us, the children will be taken care of at little or no financial disruption to my brother.

The instant you find out you are pregnant is when you need to name a guardian for your child. If you do not nominate the guardian, then the court will decide. Even if the court gets it right, there will be many hurt feelings along the way as one side shows how they are "better" than the other and how the other side just isn't as "good" as they are. No need for this. What a terrible legacy to leave your family and your children.

You may also wish to name someone other than the guardian as the manager of the children's money. You may have nominated the guardian because of her love for children and her willingness to do so, but she may not have the ability or inclination to handle the money. You may recall that I indicated my personal estate design nominates three people: the guardian, who is different than the money manager, who is different than the person who authorizes payments. These checks and balances assure everyone's interests are pure.

There will never be anyone as good as you and your husband in raising your children. There will never be anyone who will care for them like you would. Therefore, there is always going to be doubt in your selection of guardian. Your selection will never be 100 percent correct, but don't hesitate naming someone who is as close as possible.

You may want to take the time to write a letter to your children letting them know of your wishes for them to do certain things. Perhaps you want them to take clarinet lessons (like my wife did) or to play soccer (like I did). You may want them to attend a certain high school or college or pursue a certain major and course of study. I would want the children to grow up in my faith, so this would be included in the letter. I would caution you to not make this letter overreaching, but supportive of them with insights from you. You can make this letter part of your will.

Review your will often. Relationships change, people move, family members get divorced. The naming of a guardian is critical and is not a "make-it-and-forget-it" decision.

Health Care Directive, Advance Directive, Living Will

Depending on the state where you live, these documents do the same thing, but they just have different names. This important document expresses your wishes as to the medical treatment to your body if you are unable to make these decisions for yourself. This is sadly the Terri Schiavo situation. For reasons the general public was not aware of, Terri was in a vegetative state. Her husband said she would not want to live like this. Her parents said she was responding and they would care for her. However, no one knew what *Terri* wanted.

What do you want? Do you want extraordinary measures to intervene to keep you alive? Do you want a feeding tube, breathing machine, other medical care? Do you want your religious beliefs honored? Who do you want making these decisions for you?

How about your organs? Have you considered anatomical gifting, or the gifting of your body for scientific research or study?

I know there are strong beliefs with these decisions, but unless you properly express them in writing, your important wishes will not be known by others, and a judge may have to step in.

The health care directive has no power while you are able to make decisions for yourself. It only comes into power when you are unable to make them.

Durable Power of Attorney

As the health care directive nominates your agent to make medical decisions for your person (your body), the Durable Power of Attorney takes care of all your other decisions. There are a couple of different powers with this type of document.

General Powers

You have the ability to direct general power to someone "to become you" for decisions financial and otherwise. They can have the power to sell property, open

You have the ability to direct general power to someone "to become you" for decisions financial and otherwise.

accounts, enter into binding contracts (that bind you), and perform all matters you can. This is a general power, and you should be careful as to whom you give this to.

Here is an idea. You may wish to create this document and give the power to a family member or even a neighbor *without* actually giving them the document. There is no requirement for you have to give them the document itself. But if you are in the hospital recovering from an illness or accident, they could then go to the location of the document and have operate on your behalf (without having to worry about them doing something while you are otherwise healthy and capable).

Limited Powers

You can give limited powers to perform very narrow functions or larger numbers of functions as you choose. For example, you can give authority to your neighbor to sell your home, and that is it. Let's say for some reason, you move out of the local area and your home still has not yet sold. You give your neighbor limited power to sell your house (I did this when Robin was going through her cancer treatments in Massachusetts and our home needed to be sold in Colorado).

You can also give limited power to perform for a certain period of time until a certain date or event and then the power expires. For example, my best friend granted me power while he and his family were out of the country. After they returned, the power expired.

Springing Powers

Springing power comes into being only at certain predetermined events. Let's say that you create a springing power if you develop Alzheimer's disease. This power is dormant until/unless you develop this disease. You could give springing power for any measurable event and then limit this power until another measurable event. For example, you could give power if you are recovering from a surgery and this power ends when you are discharged from the hospital.

There is great flexibility with powers of attorney, and there is great risk of misuse. Be careful who you give this power to.

No matter which kind you have, durable powers can only be created while you have the ability to make an independent decision. Their powers end at your death.

There is no ownership by the person who has the power; they just have the ability to function on your behalf.

Titling

In addition to the estate planning documents mentioned above, you need to be aware of the impact as to how you own your assets. Without thinking about it, all of the assets that we have are somehow "owned" by us. From the informal ownership of our personal goods, like jewelry, TV sets, furniture, and clothes, to the formal ownership of the title of the home, car, checking accounts, and brokerage accounts, these assets are owned by us and at our passing, these assets will become owned by our survivors.

In my years of financial planning, one of the most overlooked aspects of owning assets is how they are titled. When you go to the bank, you often don't give any thought to the banker's question, "How would you like to title the account?" No matter how much thought you put into the answer, how you answer this seemingly innocuous question has *significant impact* as to how that account will be handled at incapacitation or death.

Here are the ways assets are owned and how they will

pass when one of the owners dies. Pay particular attention to this as you may want to revisit your ownership options after having a better understanding as to how they will transfer to your beneficiaries.

Joint Title

The most common titled asset among married couples is Joint Tenants with Rights of Survivorship (JTWRS). The method of titling can also be used with a parent and child, business partnership, or with other relationships. As the title suggests, joint ownership means both owners have an unlimited right to withdraw the money and the survivor will receive the money at the time the other owner dies. JTWRS ownership bypasses the probate process. By operation of law, this asset is immediately available to the joint owner regardless of the value. JTWRS assets <u>are not</u> governed by the will or the trust.

> Joan was a widowed mother of three daughters. Her estate was worth approximately $900,000, and $600,000 of it was liquid (in other words, in a variety of cash or near cash holdings such as CDs, money markets, savings and checking accounts). The balance of her estate was in the value of her house, car, and some jewelry.

> To avoid moving to a nursing home, Joan moved in with the daughter who lived nearby. The other two daughters lived across the country. Out of convenience, Joan titled all her banking assets so that the daughter she lived with could easily effect any changes, renew the CDs, and write checks, should Joan become incapacitated. Therefore, $600,000 was in joint accounts.

> Joan's desire was to divide her estate equally in thirds among her three daughters. After she died, however, "by operation of law," all the joint assets immediately went to the daughter whose name was on the accounts. The house, car, and jewelry were sold, generating $300,000 in cash, which was put into an estate account. As the estate account is governed by the will, each

daughter received her third (or $100,000) from that account. So one daughter received $700,000 and the other two received $100,000 each. This is not what Joan had intended.

The situation could have easily been avoided if (1) Joan had given the one daughter Durable Power of Attorney to help with the bank accounts or (2) Joan had placed on her accounts a Transfer on Death (TOD) to her three daughters, which would have bypassed probate, or (3) Joan had placed her liquid assets in a Revocable Living Trust and named her three daughters as equal beneficiaries. The trust would have bypassed probate as well. Any one of the three options would have ensured Joan's wishes would have been followed. This titling is not governed by the will.

Tenancy in Common

This titling is used when two or more people own the account. They can be related like a husband and wife, or father and son, but they need not be. Each owner owns a proportionate share of the account value. Because each owns his or her own share, each person has the right to sell their share, give it away, or will it upon their death. This is governed by the will.

Tenancy by the Entirety

This account ownership is only available to married couples. Neither owner can dispose of his or her half while alive without the permission of the other. Upon the death of the first, then the other becomes the sole owner. The will and trust do not govern this account.

Single Name

As the name suggests, accounts in single name are yours only. These accounts become part of the estate and are not governed by the trust. They are governed by the will.

TOD/POD

If you have added the Transfer on Death (TOD) designation, then this asset will transfer on your death to the named beneficiary. While alive, the named beneficiary has no access to the money and is not entitled to being notified that he or she is even named. At the death of the owner, this account will transfer directly to that named person. In some states, the designation is POD (Payable on Death) and this performs the same function. TOD accounts are available on most deposit accounts, brokerage accounts, and other accounts that deal with money. TOD accounts <u>are not</u> governed by the will.

CAUTION: There are cases when mothers will jointly put their only child on accounts because, "He is going to get it anyway." So the mother and son now have a joint account. Well, if the son gets into any trouble at all – divorce, lawsuit, or IRS trouble, for example – then this entire joint asset can be attached as an asset of the son as part of the son's amount of the judgment. Perhaps a better way to proceed is to give the son a Durable Power of Attorney over this account and have the account title TOD to the son or have the account in a revocable trust. This way, if the son experiences any trouble, he doesn't "own" the asset; therefore, it cannot be attached. At the mother's death, the TOD will transfer it to him and bypass probate.

Trust

Property can be titled in the name of the trust. These accounts are governed by the trust and not by the will. The executor/executrix has no authority over these accounts. Only the successor trustee will be able to settle trust accounts.

Trusts are powerful legal documents that help with the flow of assets in a specific direction under certain conditions. The trust can also be used to capture important tax savings.

NOTE: Not everybody needs a trust, and some lawyers (who get paid to write them) will be more than happy to sell you one. Please see Chapter 13, Trusts Made Easy for a complete discussion.

Pour-over Will

If you have decided that you want all of your assets to be distributed by the trust, you will want to have a "pour-over" will.

At your death, each item you own will either transfer by operation of law or will be added to your estate and be probated (see the next section on how assets are passed to heirs). When all of your assets are accounted for, those assets governed by your estate, and hence your will, should be "poured over" into the trust after the probate process concludes. By having a "pour-over" provision, you are ensuring any assets not specifically titled into the trust will still be distributed as if they were in the trust in the first place.

You would not want a pour-over will if you wanted assets to go in multiple directions. For example, if you have two or more trusts, each transferring assets in different directions, then you don't want a pour-over will. You would have taken particular care to title specific assets into specific trusts. Additionally, if you wanted only certain assets to transfer through the trust, and the rest of the assets to transfer through the estate, you would not want a pour-over provision.

> Mildred loved both children equally. She had created a trust that gives all of her assets equally to her children outright without any delay. To make sure that she didn't miss anything, she created a pour-over will to redirect all of her assets to her trust. This way, if there was an account out there she forgot about, or if she had assets that were unable to be titled (like jewelry or art), then they would all be governed by the trust because the estate was poured-over into it.

Gloria belonged to many organizations, many for pleasure and some for philanthropic reasons. She was on the board of several charities and planned to leave a substantial amount of money to them. As is with many families, Gloria has some concerns about some of her heirs and wants to set up different distributions for her children and grandchildren. She created three trusts: one for the children, the other for the grandchildren, and the third for her charities. Gloria does not want to have a pour-over will as there is more than one direction her assets are going (because she has three trusts). She has taken great care to title all of her assets into one of the three trusts, creating separate brokerage accounts, changing the beneficiaries on her life insurance and her IRA. If she acquires a new asset not titled into one of the trusts or if she overlooked something in her planning, she may not want to automatically pour-over this asset. It might be best for this to be governed by the estate and the will.

How Assets Pass to Heirs

Now that we have a better understanding of the important documents and the titling of assets that are part of a well-thought-out estate plan, let's spend a moment talking about how your assets will transfer to your heirs.

Remember the Ringling Brothers, Barnum & Bailey Circus? The one I went to had the three circular areas on the circus floor where performers would display their tricks. My favorite show was the flying trapeze show. You remember how one performer would be on the left side, swing out, and the one on the right side would time his swing so as to catch the other. There were twists, flips, and death-defying jumps. It was great. If one of the stunts missed, then the performer would fall and be caught by the net. Even that "fall" ended up being theatrical at some level.

With the trapeze in mind, picture that when someone dies, all of their assets start falling toward the net. If there is a named beneficiary, like in a provision of a life insurance policy or IRA, then one of the trapeze performers will swing out and grab that asset and give it to the named

With the trapeze in mind, picture that when someone dies, all of their assets start falling toward the net.

beneficiary. If there is a TOD designation on an account, then the performer will swing out there and grab that account. Same thing will happen to the joint accounts. For assets named into the trust, the performer will swing out there and grab them as well and put them in the keepsake box before it is locked shut. (See page 160 and the discussion on trust to understand my use of the keepsake box.)

Eventually, the flying trapeze performer will grab all of the assets designated to go somewhere. The remaining assets not "grabbed" away, will fall to the net. In this example, the net is the will. All of the other assets transferred to beneficiaries *before* they hit the will.

Many clients think the will governs all of their assets, not true. It only governs the assets that "fall" to it. Others think they don't have to worry about anything if they have created a trust. Not true. Only those assets titled into the trust will be governed by it.

I have found remarkable success with this simple analogy. People come up to me and say, "Now I get it." Send me an email and let me know if this worked for you.

Thoughts

Contractual investments (life insurance, annuities) and retirement plans (IRA, 401(k), 403(b), SEP, Roth IRA, Keogh, SIMPLE IRA, 457 Plan, Pension Plans) will transfer to the named beneficiary. If no named beneficiary is alive, the money will transfer to the contingent beneficiary. If no named or contingent beneficiary is alive, the money will fall to the estate and transfer through probate according to the will.

Titling will determine how assets will transfer. Joint ownership transfers to joint owner(s) in equal shares as to the number of joint owners. TOD and POD go to the named individual(s) in equal shares. Single ownership transfers via the will.

Assets titled into the trust will be distributed via trust instructions (and restrictions).

Your estate planning documents and the way you title your accounts will be one of the most important components of your plan while alive or at death. You can work hard at earning money, creating it through investments, safeguarding against bad decisions, but all for naught, if you don't have estate planning documents in place or if your accounts are titled incorrectly. Please see your professional team to determine if your documents are updated based on today's laws and if they will indeed transition your assets and your legacy the way you intend.

———

Your estate planning documents and the way that you have titled your accounts will be one of the most important components of your plan while alive or at your death.

———

Part Two

In-Depth Look at Investments

*There is no medicine like hope, no incentive so great and
no tonic so powerful as expectation of something tomorrow.*
Orison S. Marden

In the first part of this book, we looked at essential ingredients needed to create your financial recipe. We established the need to consider your legacy and what life lessons you will leave to your heirs. We looked at the need to determine your goals, to identify where you are going and what type of legacy you are going to leave. The first part shows you how to implement your desires with your professional team. Many of your desires will need to be expressed through your estate planning documents. We covered the risk involved and understand that it takes courage to create a plan. And we talked about how to use different investments along the Wayshak Pyramid® to diversify your assets and best position you to outpace inflation and hopefully increase your standard of living overtime.

Part One looked at the general concept of where to start, why to start, and the importance of working with a coordinated plan. We learned that you have to take controlled risk in order to outpace inflation and to have an increasing opportunity to outlive your money.

From here forward, we are going to explore in more detail the particulars of some of the underlying investment ingredients needed for your well-thought-out plan. You are going to learn about some wonderful ways to better understand often tricky topics with great stories you are not likely to forget.

We are going to talk about:

- The goose and the golden eggs
- Why mutual funds are like coffee cups and sheet cakes
- Why becoming a "loaner" might trap your income
- Why umbrellas will help your ingredients grow tax deferred; guardrails will keep your investments from falling off; and turkey gravy will help you understand taxes a little better
- The importance of trusts and what they have to do with Campbell soup cans and keepsake boxes. (You won't want to miss that one!)

Then we finish with common mistakes you can avoid now that you know about them, other important terms, and some investing techniques.

There's a lot to cover, and you'll have fun along the way, and when finished, you will have a much better understanding than you ever thought possible. I am sure of it!

8

Building the Foundation

Plan your work for today and every day, then work your plan.
Margaret Thatcher

As we take a closer look at some of the financial ingredients available to you and how they fit, we need to first lay the foundation your plan will be built on.

Consider what it takes to build chocolate chip cookies. I bet you never thought baking chocolate cookies was really building them. When you have the urge for cookies, you need to decide what kind of cookies you want. Let's say you settle on chocolate chip cookies. Without really thinking about it, you probably have dozens of potential recipes right there in your kitchen or certainly online. A Google search for "chocolate chip cookie recipes" revealed 3,570,000 recipes. (Good news, it took only 0.360 seconds for Google to search.) Once you select the recipe you are going to use, you do a mental check to see if you have all of the ingredients.

You will need some sugar, flour, chocolate morsels, and about seven other ingredients. You can even add certain personal favorites, like nuts and extra whole morsels. You pull each of these ingredients out and put them on the counter, mix them in a bowl or two, put them on a greased baking pan, preheat the oven, have a timer ready, and put out paper bags for the cookies to cool down on. The same planning process with your life needs to be accomplished.

Now that you have thought about your goals and dreams and the type of financial recipe you are going to build for yourself, we will talk about several different types of ingredients you will need to be familiar with. We will put them out on the counter and have a discussion about what they are and what they do. Once you have identified the ingredients, you will need to follow your recipe plan, add in the ingredients, like stocks, bonds, CDs, annuities, and even cash.

You will need to place your ingredients into your "life's bowl," mix, bake, and then enjoy the results.

In our chocolate chip recipe, there is no need to describe what flour is. We don't need to understand what an egg is. Vanilla extract, salt, brown sugar, butter, and baking soda don't need to be explained. I am pretty confident you know exactly what to do when the recipe calls for you to preheat the oven to 375 degrees.

But how confident are you when you hear "asset allocation?" Do you know what the ingredient bonds are for? How about stocks, mutual funds, or annuities? These and other ingredients are critical if you are to successfully follow your financial recipe.

You have heard and maybe even yourself said, "Don't put all of your eggs in one basket." Let's spend some time talking about different possible "eggs" (or ingredients) – assets – that are available to put in your financial basket.

Cash and Cash Equivalents

The foundation of an investment plan is cash. You could call it your core ingredient.

When most people think about cash, they don't think of it as an investment. Well, it certainly is. Cash is most often placed on deposit in a bank in the form of a checking, savings, or certificates of deposit (CD) accounts. A checking account has daily liquidity but low or no interest. Some are even charging a fee for the privilege to have one! Money market accounts generally have higher returns than a checking account but can be somewhat restricted in access, either by number of checks written per month or by a certain minimum amount per check. Most savings accounts pay very little interest any more. If you have any savings accounts, check with your banker to see if a money market account would be better.

Well, historically, you lose purchasing power and barely (if ever) even remain level with inflation when you buy CDs.

One of the most overused cash equivalents is the CD, the certificate of deposit. Many women put money in CDs thinking that's the best way to keep money "safe." Well, historically, you lose purchasing power and barely (if ever) even remain level with inflation when you buy CDs. Just a few short years ago, the bank was paying around one percent on one-year CDs, and inflation was nearly two percent (see chart in Charts and Tables section in the back of the book). After paying taxes, the "safe investment" lost purchasing power.

Bonds[1]

Bonds represent debt or an I.O.U. These I.O.U.'s are issued by governments (federal, state, county, or municipal) or corporations. You loan your money to the issuer, and they promise to give you periodic interest (often twice a year) and your money back at maturity.

Generally, little chance for wealth creation exists when it comes to bonds (as they are designed to return your money at maturity). Bonds are generally issued with a thirty-year maturity. A CD is essentially a short-term bond. (You loan your money to the bank, and the bank promises to pay you interest earned and return your money at maturity.)

What does it mean to be "issued"? When a company or government needs to raise money, they will issue (or sometimes you will hear it said, "float") a bond. In Northern Virginia where I live, we have quite the congestion when it comes to traffic. Recently, the county government came up with a plan to build several new roads and to widen some existing ones. These projects need to be done now, but like most municipalities, they don't have the money just sitting around for these improvements. They will need to borrow money to pay for the project. In order to borrow the money, the county issued a bond for nearly $150 million maturing in thirty years.

When these bonds were "issued," investors considered the length of time, the amount of the interest rate, the strength of the underlying issuer (Fairfax County, Virginia) and decided if they want to loan their money to the county, for a promise from the county to pay interest on time and to repay the principal at maturity.

Municipal bonds are issued by states or local government authorities. You will see bonds issued to build city streets, schools, and water treatment plants, just to name a few examples.

There are generally two types of municipal bonds: revenue and general. A major benefit to buying municipal bonds is that their dividends can be tax free. (Be certain to check with your accountant for your unique circumstances as there are some exclusions to this general rule.)

Revenue bonds are backed by revenue created by the project or whatever the bond is financing. For example, let's say there is a water treatment plant being built. That plant will receive revenue from homeowners. The bonds are then backed by the revenue generated from those homeowners.

General obligation bonds are backed by the tax base of the issuing authority. Let's say your city needs a new high school. As general obligation bonds are sold to the public, the tax base, usually through property tax, is used to guarantee the timely payment of interest owed and the return of principal at maturity.

Many municipal bonds are issued with insurance coverage by a third party insurance company. With insurance, if the revenue or general obligation bond defaults and is unable to pay, the insurance company will step in and meet the obligation.

Corporate bonds are issued by corporations to fund capital projects of the company. They are also generally issued for thirty years. A well established secondary market exists for many corporate (and municipal) bonds, giving them daily liquidity. Corporate bonds also typically pay semiannually. Unlike municipal bonds, interest payments are taxable to the recipient. Because they are taxable, corporate bonds normally pay a higher interest rate. For example, if your local bank is looking to build more branch offices, they can issue a bond to generate money enough to build those branches. The bond is only as strong as that issuer's (in this case the bank's) promise to repay.

---

[1]Bonds contain interest rate risk (as interest rates rise bond prices usually fall); the risk of issuer default; and inflation risk. The municipal market is volatile and can be significantly affected by adverse tax, legislative or political changes and the financial condition of the issuers of the municipal securities. Interest rate increases can cause the price of a debt security to decrease. A portion of the dividends you receive may be subject to federal, state, or local income tax or may be subject to the federal alternative minimum tax. A portion of a bond mutual fund's income may be subject to state taxes, local taxes and the federal alternative minimum tax.

Strength of Bonds

Third-party companies rate the underlying strength of the issuer. The rating agencies look at the factors surrounding the issuer, such as their financial strength, cash flow, tax base, corporate productivity, and the likelihood of being able to fund obligations. After looking at all aspects financial, the agencies issue a rating. The highest rating is AAA or A++, depending on the rating agency. Any rating below BBB+ is considered to be below investment grade and is commonly known as "junk."

Coupon Rates

When a bond is issued, the coupon rate is set based on market conditions at that time. If the Federal Reserve lowers the interest rates, then new bonds will be issued at lower coupon rates. If they raise the rates, the new bonds will have a higher rate. In the case of corporate bonds (bonds issued by corporations), the strength of the company will have a major impact in the determination of the interest rate. The stronger the company, the more likely they will be able to honor their guarantee, the lower the coupon rate will be. The weaker the company and therefore less likely to honor their guarantee, the higher coupon they will have to pay in order to get you to invest with them. Once issued, the coupon rate is locked in and will not change.

Call Provision

When the bond is issued, many often will have a call provision. The details of the call provision are established at issue. These details give the underlying issuer the ability to "call" away your bond at full price. To illustrate this, consider your home mortgage. When you purchased your home, you probably used a thirty-year mortgage to help you finance so you could move in. If during those thirty years, interest rates drop and it becomes favorable for you to refinance, you would "call" away your mortgage and refinance at a lower rate. Generally, the mortgage company can't prevent you from paying off the mortgage early.

Same with a bond. If they issue the bond, for example, at 6% coupon and the rates drop to 4%, the issuer will want to refinance and will call away their higher paying bond and replace it with a lower paying one. Just like your mortgage company, if there is a call provision, you can't prevent them from doing this. They will refund your money in full and stop paying you the 6%. You would then decide if you wanted a new bond, or something completely different.

Interest Rate Risk

When your bond matures or is called away, there is a risk that the new rates will be lower than what you were receiving. In the above example, the issuer called the bond when the rates dropped and it made financial sense for them to do so. On the other hand, you lose the higher 6% rate and can only invest it in a new lower 4% rate. The loss of interest earned is considered interest rate risk. What's worse, if you went all thirty years, you would only get your principal back without growth, the cost of goods and services would have increased (due to inflation) and your new rate of interest could be even lower.

What's worse, if you went all thirty years, you would only get your principal back without growth, the cost of goods and services would have increased (due to inflation) and your new rate of interest could be even lower.

Price Fluctuations

Even though the coupon rate will not change once issued, the underlying price of the bond will change.

NOTE: There are many reasons for bond price fluctuation. Some to consider are the issuer's ability to keep their promise to pay interest and principal at maturity. Change in consumer spending habits that can change the tax base (for municipal bonds) or could change the desire for the company product (like Enron). Management changes can impact the quality of the issuing company/municipality that will in turn impact the price. Remember, most bonds are issued for thirty years and a lot can occur during this time.

Of course, during those thirty years, interest rates will fluctuate up and down. This movement will have an inverse effect on the value of bonds already issued. Remember, there are other factors affecting the price of bonds, but if we consider only interest rate movements, as long term interest rates rise, the underlying value of bonds will fall. If interest rates decrease, then bonds will tend to increase in value.

Let me give you an example:

> Let's say you purchased a bond several years ago for $100,000 and it's paying you a 5 percent coupon rate. Let's further say the Federal Reserve has lowered rates and new bonds issued are paying 4 percent. You decide you want to sell your bond. You find a buyer who is willing to buy a new 4 percent bond from me for $100,000 and you have a nice, attractive 5 percent bond you are willing to sell. If the buyer can only get 4 percent from me with a new purchase, and you have a 5 percent, then you will sell yours to him for a premium. Perhaps you will sell your bond to him for $105,000! You would then earn a $5,000 profit.

> The opposite can be true. Let's say you bought your bond with a coupon of 5 percent and interest rates fluctuate up and new bonds are paying 6 percent. You need to sell. Your bond is less attractive than the new one, therefore the buyer is not going to pay you full price for your bond, but will pay you a discount. Maybe you will only get $95,000.

> Many clients will say, "But if the principal is guaranteed, how can I get less back?" The principal is guaranteed *at maturity*. If you sell early, you will be subject to all the risks associated with bonds, including interest rate risk for premature sells.

NOTE: Even federal government bonds (which are backed by the full faith and taxing power of the government) can be sold at a loss, if interest rates go up and the holder sells early. *Nothing is "safe" and guaranteed to return your principal at all times under every situation.* This doesn't mean you shouldn't invest in bonds; it just means you should realize bonds have risks as well as other investments.

The Goose and the Golden Eggs

When we deal with bonds, you need only to think about a goose and the golden eggs. When you buy a bond, you need to decide if you are an egg collector or a goose trader. As just described, bonds have a promised semi-annual interest payment. These payments I consider to be the golden eggs. As we also know, the value of bonds will fluctuate with interest market movements and other factors. I consider these bonds to be the goose. The vast majority of bond buyers are looking for consistent, secure periodic payments and want to collect golden eggs. They are not overly concerned about the underlying price of the goose.

> *If you are going to collect eggs, don't worry yourself when the price changes and the value on your statement is below what you paid for them. Just collect the eggs and enjoy.*

You should decide *before* you buy a bond if you are looking to collect the golden eggs (get a consistent income stream) or if you are looking to be a goose trader and take advantage of bond price fluctuations. If you are going to collect eggs, don't worry yourself when the price changes and the value on your statement is below what you paid for them. Just collect the eggs and enjoy.

Stocks

There are several different kinds of stocks companies can issue. For our general discussion here, we are only going to talk only about common stocks. Common stocks are shares of ownership of the issuing company.

As an owner, you have the right to vote your shares and earn profits in the form of dividends and capital appreciation. Capital appreciation is explained as the price per share climbing from where you bought it, say $20 per share, to where you sell it, say $31 per share. In this case, there would be an $11 capital appreciation per share. Companies may also declare dividends to stockholders. Many times these dividends are based on company profits. Companies can also decide to take all the profits and roll them back in for continued research, development, expansion and other reasons. The stockholder may receive both the dividend and the capital appreciation.

As an owner, you also share in the risk of loss if the stock goes in the other direction. You would then have a capital loss. We have seen recently dramatic price fluctuations. To be sure, there are many risks to owning stocks.

To also be sure, being an owner of a company (owner of their stock) has the wonderful potential for creating wealth over time.

There are other books and publications that go into greater depth about what a stock is and I would encourage you to review them if desired. Clearly this is just a brief discussion here with little detail as to the overall risk associated with stock investing. Stocks are designed to outpace inflation and give real benefit to a properly diversified portfolio. Work with your financial advisor and ask them questions about the different kinds of stocks and their associated risks.

Mutual Funds[2]

You may have heard that mutual funds are a combination of stocks and bonds managed by someone who is looking to make you money. Amongst other important qualifications, these managers are generally well trained and have years of industry knowledge. Perhaps your first exposure to mutual funds was with your company 401(k). Within the company plan, you had to choose where your money was invested. You probably looked at the historical return and picked a couple of choices that looked good. The whole process might have taken you five minutes.

I often ask clients, "In your own words, describe for me what a mutual fund is." I have received some interesting answers. Over the years of being a financial advisor, I have used the following two analogies to help clients get a visual picture of what a mutual fund really is. They have repeatedly come back to me saying they finally "get it." (Let me know if this is helpful to you.)

[2]Mutual funds are sold by prospectus only. Please carefully consider investment objectives, risks, charges, and expenses before investing.

Example #1. Mutual funds are like coffee cups. Picture a coffee cup. Put the coffee cup right in front of you. Maybe it is on the end table next to your bed or the kitchen table as you're reading this book. Here is a simple question:

What can you put inside that coffee cup?

The first answers that come to mind are coffee, cream, and sugar. Some people will answer tea and others milk. All those answers are correct. You can also put in paperclips, pencils, and coins. You can even fill your coffee cup up with dirt.

The "flavor" of your coffee cup is going to depend upon its ingredients. Let's say you take a sip and it tastes like mint chocolate latté. If so, you would have a very good idea of what the underlying ingredients are. On the other hand, if you take a sip of a different cup and it tastes like dirt, well you would still have a very good idea of those ingredients.

When you think about it, a coffee cup is really just something that holds something else. The "something else" it holds gives it its flavor. Well, a mutual fund is the same thing. It is something that holds something else. The ingredients of the mutual fund give it the "flavor" (and risk - the potential for gain and loss).

> *When you think about it, a coffee cup is really just something that holds something else.*

You ask, "What do you mean by the mutual fund gets its 'flavor' based on the underlying investments added to the coffee cup?" If the mutual fund holds cash investments, it would be called a money market fund. If it holds bond investments, that would be called an income fund. If the ingredients were blue chip companies, you would have a blue chip stock fund.

128

Many times, you can get a strong sense as to the ingredients based in part on the name of the fund. If the fund is called "government bond fund," well then you would have a sense that the ingredients are underlying government securities such as treasury bills, treasury bonds, and other government-issued debts and bonds. On the other hand, if your mutual fund says "international stocks," right away you'd know that the ingredients of your mutual fund are stocks of international companies.

I have had prospects ask me, "What are your mutual funds earning?" I answer them, "It depends on what flavor are you talking about!"

Example #2. Mutual funds are also like sheet cakes. If I were to ask you to bake me a vanilla sheet cake from scratch, you would preheat the oven and start gathering the ingredients. Of those ingredients, you would include eggs, milk, flour, sugar, vanilla, salt, and others. You would mix them together, grease the pan, pour, and bake.

When the cake was finished, if I asked you to cut me a large piece, the percentage of ingredients in that large piece would be the same as if I asked you to cut me a small piece. Both pieces would have the same percentage of those eggs, milk, flour, and other ingredients. The "size" of the piece does not determine how much of one ingredient I have over another. The percentage is determined by how much of that ingredient you put in the mixing bowl in the first place.

A mutual fund is the same. No matter if you start investing with a modest amount or buy thousands of dollars worth, you will receive the same percentage of the underlying ingredients. You will therefore be completely diversified within that mutual fund, regardless of the amount invested.

The mutual fund is managed by the company that puts the fund together. That company has a baker (portfolio manager) who determines the ingredients (typically stocks or bonds, but can be almost any type of security) based on the recipe (prospectus) and flavor (risk tolerance) of the fund.

Clients have told me they were not interested in buying stocks. They just wanted to buy growth mutual funds. Interesting enough, when you buy growth mutual funds, you are indeed buying stocks. You see, the underlying mutual fund is itself buying stocks, so when you buy that mutual fund, you are buying <u>what it buys</u>. So when that client says, "I don't want to buy any stocks," I always have to clarify if they mean individual stocks or if we can buy them through mutual funds.

Thoughts

Now that we have a sense of cash, stocks, bonds, and mutual funds, we now have a foundation as to how these items can be mixed together to help build your plan. This may sound silly, but you have to have a sense of cotton before you can understand thread which is stitched into a blouse. The same is true about cash put together to form a CD, money market or checking account. Same as stocks and bonds that are put together to form mutual funds. These ingredients have different risks that need to be considered when mixed to create your plan. Coming up next we are going to discuss how they fit into asset classes.

Now that we have a sense of cash, stocks, bonds, and mutual funds, we now have a foundation as to how these items can be mixed together to help build your plan.

9

Understanding Asset Classes

*I would like to invest in a nice, honest, wholesome company
that makes obscene profits.*
Wall Street Wit & Wisdom

As we continue to lay the foundation of your financial recipe, we need to see how some of those ingredients we talked about earlier in "Building the Foundation" start fitting together to form asset classes. There are different asset classes that cover the entire spectrum of potential investment risk, from the lowest level of risk to the highest.

When investing, risk is needed to outpace inflation and keep you even with purchasing power. Risk is like cholesterol - a little is required for energy, but a lot can be dangerous. Asset classes can be summarized into five basic risk categories going from Cash, the lowest level of risk to Aggressive Growth, the most risk:

- Cash
- Income
- Growth and Income
- Growth
- Aggressive Growth

These classes of investments were introduced to you on page 53 when we discussed the Wayshak Pyramid®. Here, let's spend a little more time talking about each asset class in a little more detail.

Cash[1]

We have already spoken about cash as one of the ingredients used in your financial plan. Cash is also one of the asset classes. There is minimal risk in the short term if money is in cash. Other investments in this asset class are savings, checking, and money market accounts. Also,

CDs and bonds coming due within the next two years are generally considered to be in the cash asset class.

Income[1]

The income class does not represent the income you earn but the income the investment earns. This class is full of income producing assets, usually bonds. This asset class obviously generates income, but it provides little long term growth, if any.

Every category has their risks and some of the income risk associated here is due to ups and downs of the interest rate market, default risk of the bond issuer, and reinvestment risk, to name a few. The reinvestment risk is the risk that interest rates will be lower when the bond comes due. Your new investment may then generate a lower income. When your original investment is repaid back to you in full, there is an inflation risk your principal will have decreased in purchasing value.

Growth and Income[1]

Growth and income investments provide some room for growth and some reasonable amount of income. Usually, ingredients in this category are mature stock companies paying high dividends that still have room for growth. Some growth and income mutual funds will have 50 percent of the assets in growth-related stocks and 50 percent of the assets in bonds, hence growth and income.

Because 'growth' has been introduced, risk has increased. Generally, when you hear "growth" as an investment option, you need to hear "stocks", and with that, all of the associated risks.

Growth[1]

Growth-oriented investments are designed to provide capital appreciation, where the stock price is hopefully going to go up. Growth companies generally direct their profits back into the company for continued growth, capital improvements, research, and development.

Growth companies, if they do well, will give strong returns over time. There will generally be low or no dividends and, therefore, little cash flow to the investor. The goal of growth investing is to grow your original principal and when you sell it, sell it for more than you bought it for, then enjoy the capital gain.

The risk level is increasing here. There must be consideration of potential negative returns. Remember the Wayshak Pyramid®, you need to have a willingness to hold the investment for a long term period before you invest here. All portfolios are dependent on the individual's needs and goals, but as an investor ages and moves forward along their life cycle, the number of investments in this category will generally decline.

Aggressive Growth[1]

This asset class is for the speculative portion of the portfolio. This class has small companies looking to grow and become the next Wal-Mart or IBM. This category of companies I jokingly refer to as "Bill Gates and Microsoft when they were still in his garage."

Aggressive growth will also include overseas companies where the risk is increased. Whenever you invest overseas, you not only are dealing with the company and its ability to earn a profit, but you are exposed to currency movements, government regulations, and political instability.

Here in this category, the risk level is at the highest point. Please be careful when you place your money in aggressive growth investments. You will most likely have the least amount of assets in this category.

NOTE: There are exceptions to every rule. Where bonds are normally considered to have certain downside risk protection and normally fall into the income asset class, not all of them do. Consider junk bonds. These investments are bonds and are backed by the issuer for timely payment of interest owed and repayment of principal at maturity. And they can be very risky (hence the word *junk*) and fall into the aggressive category.

[1] There is no assurance that any investment strategy will be successful. Investing involves risk and you may incur a profit or a loss.

General Returns Over Time

Over my years as a financial advisor, I have been asked to "guesstimate" the returns of money in the different asset categories. I do not have any hard and fast data, but I believe for planning purposes the chart shown here can give you a sense of the potential returns in the various different categories. Here is a *very* broad expectation of returns based on the level of risk you are willing and able to take. You need to be aware these numbers are representative over time. In any given year, the numbers could be much higher or lower as the case may be. One of the trickiest components of a financial advisor's job is setting realistic expectations. Understanding potential returns can assist in setting your objectives. In the past several years, interest rates have been historically very low.

Asset class	Expected return over time
Cash (savings and money markets)	2–4%
CDs	4–5%
Income (taxable bonds)	5–6%
Growth and Income	7–8%
Growth	8–10%
Aggressive Growth	10–12%

If you look at all the charts and all the historical measures, you will see that the previous numbers have been close over time. Yes, there are periods of higher returns and periods of lower returns for all the risk categories, but averaged together, this is what I feel comfortable in planning for client's return. There has only been one period of time that the market hasn't been higher ten years later. That was in 1972 when the Dow Jones Industrial Average (the Dow, which is reported every evening on the news) crossed 1,000 points for the first time. Ten years later in 1982, it crossed 1,000 points for the last time and kept climbing. Although the market didn't move during this time, many companies still paid a dividend so there was positive return on your investment. And, if you reinvested those dividends, you would have an even greater return!

Remember, the goal for your plan is not to become rich (although that would be nice); your goal is not to become poor or lose purchasing power.

Thoughts

Each asset class has its own potential risk and its own potential reward. You will want to consider carefully your situation and the time horizon you have before you develop the proper allocation for your investments. Rely on your financial advisor to help guide you and always consider there is no real reason to take too much risk!

This might be a good time to go back to the Wayshak Pyramid® and review. Some of the earlier discussions may now become clearer with the additional information.

---

*Rely on your
financial advisor to help
guide you and always
consider that there is no
real reason to take too
much risk!*

10

Loaner vs. Owner

Do you know the only thing that gives me pleasure? It's to see my dividends coming in.

John D. Rockefeller

As we are talking about the different ingredients in which to invest money, we also need to discuss whether we "own" those investments or if we "loan" them. Think of where you live. Do you own your home or are you renting? If you are renting, who is creating wealth, you the tenant or the landlord?

As you consider the need to diversify your money, it is critical that you grow part of the money. It is so easy to let your investments sit on deposit in a CD or savings account, but this type of decision provides no growth and little opportunity to keep even with inflation. You need to grow some of your money by being an owner and not just a loaner.

Basically, you have two choices when it comes to investing money. You can either lend it to someone or some company or you can buy ownership with the purchase of an asset, such as a stock, a home, or a painting. Real wealth is created and maintained with ownership.

Loan It

You may have never thought about this as a loan, but when you go to the bank and deposit your money, you are indeed lending your money to them. When you get a CD, you are lending your money to the bank for the period of time, say twelve months, and they promise to pay you back all of your money at maturity and the interest you've earned. You do the same thing with checking, savings, and money market accounts.

Of course when you buy a bond of any kind, you are lending your money to the company or municipality that issued the bond. They promise to pay the par value (face value) of the bond at maturity and timely payment of interest owed to you along the way.

You may never have thought about it, but what do companies do with the money you loan them? Companies might use this borrowed money to build a plant they would now own for future productivity for their company. This new plant will increase their assets and, translated, will give the company even more ownership. Wouldn't it be great if you could be an owner?

With "loan" money, you are getting interest along the way and your money back at maturity. But your *purchasing power* has been negatively affected by time and inflation. We talked a little about this earlier but here is a great *true* example.

> *But your* purchasing power *has been negatively affected by time and inflation.*

In the early 1980s, you may remember that inflation was double digits and U.S. Government treasuries were being issued at all time high interest rates! If you bought a thirty-year Treasury Bond in October 1981, you could have bought that bond with a whopping yield of 14.6 percent.* When this bond matured in 2011, the reinvested principal will earn just 3.13 percent.

If you invested $100,000 in 1981, you would be receiving $14,600 a year. In 2011, you will receive your money back and when you reinvest, you will only receive $3,130 a year. What's worse, because of the impact of inflation, your purchasing power will have declined. In order to duplicate the purchasing power of the $14,600 that you received since 1982, you need to earn $36,128 in 2011.** Purchasing power risk is real. This is a tremendous risk to you from what you may have thought was an otherwise "safe" investment.

*http://research.stlouisfed.org/fred2/data/GS30.txt

**http://data.bls.gov/cgi-bin/cpicalc.pl

Loan investments should be a part of your portfolio, but it should only be that part you need to feel comfortable. Rarely does a properly diversified portfolio have all money in loan investments. Because of the risk in losing purchasing power, you should give great consideration in growing part of your investments. By being a loaner, you greatly increase your chance of becoming trapped with fixed income payments. That would mean you are now on a "fixed income" in a time of need for increasing income due to inflation.

Own It

Yes, you can own a bond or CD, but you are really lending your money to the issuing bond company or to the bank. Real wealth is created with true ownership. You can either own your own company or own your assets outright. Or you can own companies and assets through individual stock or mutual funds. Because you own, you partake in the profits. You have the ability to gain wealth. You can begin to outpace inflation and increase your purchasing power.

As great as ownership sounds, when you own, you also share in the potential loss. You can come out of that investment with less than what you put in. It is even possible you may end up with nothing at all. That's why you diversify.

Is it better to rent when you can own? Many will tell you that owning is better. Yes, there are always the horror stories, but the vast majority of people who own, over time, end up better off owning than with any other decision they could have made.

It is even possible that you may end up with nothing at all. That's why you diversify.

One of the most popular ways to own investments is through stock mutual funds. The diversification within gives certain downside protection and the gain over time should give upside purchasing power. As companies distribute cash to the owners, these are dividends, not interest, representing a share of the profits, not a repayment of a debt owed.

Remember earlier we talked about how the stock market was flat for the ten years from 1972 to 1982. On November 14, 1972, the Dow crossed 1,000 points for the first time[1] and on December 17, 1982 it crossed 1,000 for the last time[2]. If you owned a growth and income fund[3] during that time and had reinvested the dividends, you would have earned 8.9 percent on average each year. As companies you owned within the mutual fund paid dividends, those dividends were then reinvested buying more shares.

Thoughts

Certainly past performance does not indicate future gain, but owning assets, even those through mutual funds or ETFs, can provide for a better potential future than if you loaned your money.

[1]http://www.djindexes.com/mdsidx/index.cfm?event=showavgDecades&decade=1970
[2]http://www.djindexes.com/mdsidx/index.cfm?event=indexHistory
[3]American Funds, "The ICA Guide" 2007 Investor's Guide, page 16.

11

Individual Retirement Account (IRA), 401(k), 403(b), 457, SEPP, Keogh, and Any Other Qualified Retirement Plan

Don't simply retire from something; have something to retire to.
Harry Emerson Fosdick

Federal law allows each worker in the United States with a valid social security number to have a retirement account. Current law allows the employee to participate with a company retirement plan, or to have one on their own, sometimes both.

The only way you can contribute to the retirement plan is if you have earned income or are married to a working spouse. You cannot contribute to a retirement plan if you don't have earned income. For example, if you receive money from a trust, dividends from a partnership, most rental property, social security, or investments, to name a few, that money is not considered to be earned income.

Retirement plans come in two different broad categories: defined benefit or defined contributions.

- Defined benefit plans are becoming increasingly rare. These are like pension plans with defined benefits. For example, if you work for the company for twenty years, then the company will pay you 'x' amount at retirement for life (a defined amount). The company guarantees this benefit. Sadly, many companies have been unable to meet their obligations. You may have heard steel workers, pilots, auto manufacturers, and other companies have had to greatly adjust *down* their pension and benefit packages. This type of retirement program, the defined benefit, is not being discussed here.

- It is the defined contribution plans where you as the employee decide if you are going to contribute to the plan or not. So when I refer to a *retirement plan*, please be aware that we are discussing the defined contribution plans and not other plans, like defined benefit, pension, or stock option plans that might be available.

We need to establish that (a) the law provides for the retirement plan and (b) the company you work for decides what investments (ingredients) are available inside of the plan. Federal law allows for the employer to establish a retirement plan for the employee to contribute to. It is the employer who decides which investment company will be used for the employees to invest through.

Several types of defined contribution retirement plans are available to the average working American. These plans come from an employer/employee relationship. Said differently, these plans are funded while you are working (and many plans have wonderful benefits such as company matches). You may have heard of some of them:

- 457 Plan for government workers
- 403(b) for employees who work in nonprofit organizations, such as many hospitals, schools, and churches
- 401(k)for employees in for-profit companies such as Home Depot or Wal-Mart
- SEP (Simplified Employee Pension plan) used by many self-employed workers or business owners with few employees, such as Realtors

The type of plan your company has will generally depend on the number of employees and the corporate structure (like For Profit, Not For Profit, C Corp, Partnership or Limited Liability Company – just to name a few).

No matter which type of plan the company offers, tax law generally treats these plans similarly. Therefore, for ease of discussion, I am going to explain all of them as if they were all an IRA.

NOTE: One other twist needs to be discussed. Congress created the Roth IRA as an additional savings options. You will hear discussion about the Roth IRA and the traditional IRA. For the purpose of this section, we are only going to discuss the traditional IRA, as the traditional IRA is the one taxed the same as the employer-sponsored plans.

NOTE: Important differences between the Roth and traditional IRA will impact you and your decisions regarding these different types of plans. The following discussion is meant as a guideline only. Please seek professional help for your specific needs.

I have prospects ask me, "What is your IRA paying?" This question is a great clue to me that they might not fully understand what an IRA is in the first place.

IRA stands for Individual Retirement Account. *Individual* because it can only be titled to one individual. *Retirement* because it is geared toward retirement and there is a penalty under normal circumstances if withdrawals are made before you are fifty-nine-and-a-half years old. While in the IRA, the investment grows tax-deferred; this is wonderful. *Account* means your funds are held by a financial institution and can contain almost any type of investment.

But I tell my clients an IRA really is just an umbrella. Simple as that. A simple analogy using the concept of an umbrella follows. If you are outside and it's raining, the umbrella protects you from becoming wet from the rain. Inside the investment world, the umbrella protects you from becoming soaked by the taxes.

How the IRA Works

Money deposited into the IRA (deposited under the umbrella) is pretax. You either make an annual contribution or you rollover money from another plan from work, like a 401(k) or a 403(b) or other company-sponsored plan. Now that the money is under the umbrella, it is protected from being soaked by the taxes. There are no taxes of any kind, no capital gains and no income tax, as long as the money stays below the umbrella and in the IRA.

Once the money is under the umbrella, where is it invested? Great question! My answer is this: in coffee cups that are available from the institution that provided you the umbrella (as discussed earlier on page 127, under Mutual Funds).

Huh? Let me give you an example. If you walk into the local bank, they might have a placard displaying their IRA rates for CD investments. They might have a twelve-month rate or an eighteen month rate, for example. Well, if you deposit money into their IRA, you have used their IRA umbrella to shelter you from the taxes, and you have used their coffee cup containing a CD for twelve or eighteen months.

If you walk into a different bank, then you would use their different IRA umbrella and use their different coffee cups.

If you go to a financial advisor, you would use their IRA umbrella and have the coffee cups available that they offer. The financial advisor's "cup" will contain a wide variety of choices from CDs to bonds to stocks to mutual funds and more.

Now that you know an IRA is just an umbrella, then you will quickly realize you can go to any institution that offers umbrellas. You can get your IRA from insurance companies, brokerage firms, independent financial advisors, and banks, each offering cups with different contents. Remember, federal law provides for the IRA; the company you wish to buy yours from provides the investment options. No one way is right or wrong. Just be aware of the fees and charges before you buy and the associated risk of the investment.

Spend time with your advisor and make sure the risk you take in the IRA is consistent with your overall financial plan and time horizon.

CAUTION: Be leery of the firm or financial advisor that suggests you use their proprietary products. Proprietary products are products owned by the same company that is trying to now sell them to you. I find as a general rule of thumb, proprietary products may not be as competitive as products available in the open market, and there is generally internal pressure or incentive of some kind to offer those proprietary choices.

So now when you come and ask me, "What is my IRA paying?" I am going to answer, "It depends on which coffee cup you have chosen." Refer to the next figure.

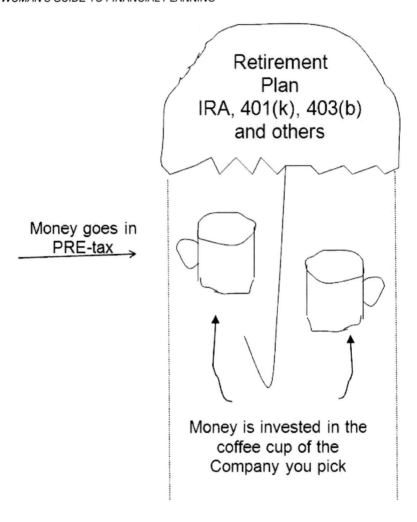

**Retirement
Plan
IRA, 401(k), 403(b)
and others**

Money goes in
__PRE-tax__ →

Money is invested in the
coffee cup of the
Company you pick

Normal Distribution Age

When you pull the money out after you are fifty-nine-and-a-half years old, there is no federal penalty for that withdrawal. There will be an income tax due at that time, based on whatever tax bracket you are in. The amount withdrawn is always taxed as ordinary income based on the rate you are in at the time you made the withdrawal. There are no capital gains or capital losses with IRAs.

If you pull out before you are fifty-nine-and-a-half years old, a 10 percent federal penalty usually is assessed on the amount you pull out, and you have to pay ordinary income taxes, *even* on that federal penalty.

Exceptions

There are some narrow exceptions allowing you to pull money out before you're fifty-nine-and-a-half. These exceptions include substantially equal periodic payments or 72(t) rule, first-time home purchases, medical expenses and for certain education expenses just to name some. Please work directly with your financial advisor if you need IRA money before you reach the magic age of fifty-nine-and-a-half.

NOTE: Qualified exceptions forgive the penalty, but you still have to pay the ordinary taxes. Review IRS Publication 590, (IRAs) for more details.

Required Minimum Distribution (RMD)

You are required by federal law to pull money out of the IRA once you reach the age of seventy-and-a-half. The first distribution is required by April 1st of the year following the year that you turn seventy-and-a-half.

Here is an example: If you were born in January and turned seventy that year, you would turn seventy-and-a-half in July. Your first payment is required by April 1st the following year. If you were born in August, you would turn seventy-and-a-half in March of the next year. You would have until April 1 of the *following* year to pull out your first required minimum distribution.

Let's look at the IRA umbrella now.

The government requires
distributions because that's the
only way it can get tax revenue
from this money.

145

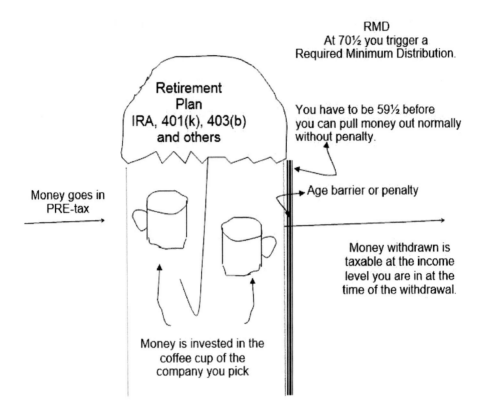

For your information: Why does the federal government *require* a distribution at all? Well, there is over $8 trillion (yes, trillion) inside retirement accounts, and not one cent of that money has yet to be taxed. The government *requires* distributions because that's the only way it can get tax revenue from this money.

The government has even been so kind as to create a convenient table for you to use, which will help you determine the amount they force you to take each year, based on your age. Here is the standard table the IRS publishes to help you determine the distribution that is required.

Uniform Table for Determining Factor Lifetime Distributions

Age at end of year	Applicable Divisor	Age at end of year	Applicable Divisor
70	27.4	93	9.6
71	26.5	94	9.1
72	25.6	95	8.6
73	24.7	96	8.1
74	23.8	97	7.6
75	22.9	98	7.1
76	22.0	99	6.7
77	21.2	100	6.3
78	20.3	101	5.9
79	19.5	102	5.5
80	18.7	103	5.2
81	17.9	104	4.9
82	17.1	105	4.5
83	16.3	106	4.2
84	15.5	107	3.9
85	14.8	108	3.7
86	14.1	109	3.4
87	13.4	110	3.1
88	12.7	111	2.9
89	12.0	112	2.6
90	11.4	113	2.4
91	10.8	114	2.1
92	10.2	115 and older	1.9

Uniform Lifetime Table 590-B (2015)

Example: You are seventy-three years old at the end of the year 2014, and your account balance of all of your IRAs was $475,000 as of 12/31/2014. You are required to pull out $19,230.77 by December 31, 2015. You will add this amount to your income for taxes owed for the year 2015, which are due by April 15, 2016.

Looking at the table, the factor at age seventy-three is 24.7.

The calculation is this: $475,000 / 24.7 = $19,230.77.

IMPORTANT: Due to recent extreme fluctuations in the stock market, Congress is considering some relief regarding Required Minimum Distributions. Consult with your advisor for any last minute legislation updates.

Please consult a qualified accountant when you are preparing your taxes.

Beneficiary

Please make sure you have a named beneficiary on all of your IRA accounts. Your named beneficiary will have some wonderful options when inheriting the money and may be able to take the money over their lifetime! This will only happen if the IRA holder named them beneficiary. Unfortunately, if the beneficiary receives this money from the estate, then they will lose the ability to stretch over their lifetime. If you have outlived your beneficiary, then immediately update to a new one.

As a general rule, you should also name a contingent beneficiary as well. If you don't, then the probate process will determine who receives this inheritance, if the primary beneficiary pre-deceases you.

Funny Story

I tell this umbrella analogy to all my clients. One of my clients returned from a cruise and shared with me that she had order one of those tropical fruit drinks. The waiter brought it to the pool side lounge chair as she was soaking in the rays. When he handed it to her, it was in one of those tall glasses filled to the rim with the drink and on top was one of those tropical umbrellas stuck into the drink. She said she couldn't stop laughing as she was thinking she was drinking from her IRA!

Thoughts

Retirement accounts can have wonderful benefits. Not only do they grow tax free, but they can be stretched by your beneficiaries. However, there are many details with these accounts. Check with your financial advisor as to how to best use your retirement account now, and within your estate plan.

12

Annuities, The Vale Removed

A large income is the best recipe for happiness I ever heard of.
Jane Austen

Now that you are familiar with coffee cups from our mutual fund definition, and you are familiar with umbrellas from the IRA definition, let's look at another potential ingredient that you may encounter on your way toward building your perfect, unique financial recipe.

Annuities are only offered through life insurance companies, and, based on current law, the growth in the annuity is tax deferred. Even though a life insurance company issues the annuity, it is not life insurance. Life insurance requires some kind of medical underwriting, like a blood sample, medical questions, and examination of medical records. Life insurance is designed to *create* an estate (at death). Annuities are designed to *spend* an estate (create income) while you are alive.

You need to be fifty-nine-and-a-half before you can pull money out of an annuity (just like your IRA), without triggering a federal penalty for early withdrawal. Whether you have to pull a RMD (required minimum distribution) is dependent upon whether the annuity was purchased with IRA or other qualified money or whether it was purchased with money from savings or nonqualified money. Let me explain.

Qualified Annuities

If you bought an annuity with retirement money, like your IRA or 401(k), then your annuity is pretax and is considered "qualified" money. This means *all* distributions will be taxed when you withdraw, and you have to wait until you are fifty-nine-and-a-half to start without penalty. You will also have an RMD at age seventy-and-a-half. Qualified annuities are taxed just like IRAs.

NOTE: A qualified annuity is simply retirement money that purchased an annuity. You can move back to a normal IRA if desired, and back to an annuity. Think of the annuity as being just one of the coffee cups underneath the IRA umbrella.

Non-Qualified Annuities

If you purchased your annuity with after tax money (not a new tax, but just not pretax) then you have a "nonqualified" annuity. You will pay taxes only on the gain. You will still need to wait until you are fifty-nine-and-a-half to pull out the gain penalty free, but there is no RMD at seventy-and-a-half.

NOTE: As you withdraw, you will pay taxes on the gain first. Once all the gain is pulled out, then you will withdraw your principal tax free.

I tell my clients an annuity is an umbrella with coffee cups protected by guardrails. The umbrella because the money grows tax deferred. The coffee cups because you decide the risk of where the money is invested under the umbrella. Guardrails because the insurance company provides certain guarantees (that can be quite attractive).

As the era of company pension plans basically ends, many investors are creating their own pension plans through insurance companies. Annuities are products the insurance companies offer that have attractive guarantees and lifetime pension-like income benefits.

Upside

In today's market, you can find annuities offering some significant guardrails (benefits). Here are just a few:

- Guaranteed return of your principal
- Lifetime income you cannot outlive
- Guaranteed step-up value to your loved ones at your death, if the current market value is lower than the guaranteed step up value

- Guaranteed increasing income that keeps pace with inflation
- Tax-free transfer within investments (you don't pay capital gains tax)
- No cost or commissions to transfer and make changes
- And others (ask your advisor)

Downside

With any program there are some downsides:

- When you have guarantees, you may have higher internal "insurance" expenses and fees. Pay attention to this. Because any money you earn but don't keep, is just like money you didn't earn in the first place.
- You typically have a surrender period. You have to hold the investment for a certain length of time in order to bypass a contractual penalty if you sell early. You will have some access to funds, generally 10 percent of the premium that can be taken out annually without company penalty. Make sure you check for early withdrawal provisions.
- If you pull money out before you are fifty-nine-and-a-half, there will normally be a federal penalty. This may also be in addition to the company penalty mentioned earlier.
- Any increase in the value of the contract is taxed as ordinary income. There are no capital gains (or losses) available with annuities. Just like in an IRA or other qualified investment, any gain is taxed at the rate you are in when you withdraw that gain.

CAUTION: If you pull out before the surrender period is over and before fifty-nine-and-a-half, you will pay a company penalty and a federal penalty and ordinary tax on any of the gain. You will even have to pay taxes on the penalty amount. Be certain that money invested in annuities is "long-term" money, and you have plenty of liquidity in other areas if you need funds *pre*-fifty-nine-and-a-half.

Many of my clients recognize the stock market is a "wealth creator," but there are periods of "wealth deflator" as well. They realize over time the market has gone up and they want to participate. On the other hand, fear of a market downturn keeps them in traditional deposit products. I consider this investor to be on the fence. An annuity could be a great fit for this type of market-leery client and help them get off the fence onto the side of the stock market. Consider the following analogy.

> Picture a major bridge, such as the Golden Gate Bridge in California. You are on this bridge and without thinking about it, you drive the speed limit (or maybe even faster). Even if the weather changes, the wind blows and it starts to rain, you might slow down, but you are going to cross it anyway. Now, in your mind, take off the guardrails. That's it. Rip them right off and let them fall to the ground (or water) below. You still have the road, it is still as strong as before, but there are no guardrails. Do you still cross it? Do you go the speed limit as you look over the side and see below?

Many times clients view the volatility of the stock market as this bridge without guardrails. Instinctively, they know that the stock market goes up, and people can make money in the market, providing for a stronger retirement. But these clients have also heard some horror stories of market crashes and people losing money.

Consider that portion of your portfolio invested for the long run. There is no guarantee, but if you can hold that money without pulling out, as earlier discussed, over a ten year period, even after the great depression, the flat decade of the 1970's, even after 9-11-2001, or the 2008 crash, I believe the odds of losing money over time are very low. If you panic and pull out, well then you will have certainly lost.

The odds of falling off a bridge are low as well. But if you intentionally strike the barrier as you drive, then you will at some point fall off. Some people are not willing to take those odds. So instead of taking advantage of the market, they just turn to deposit items and guaranteed investments (with which you don't lose money but you also don't create wealth; you barely stay even with inflation, if at all).

Clients would think differently about the stock market if they knew there was insurance against this unlikely crash. Just like the bridge, if the guardrails were up, they would think much differently about the bridge than if there were no guardrails at all.

How would you like to have the upside of the market with guardrails to protect against the market fall?

Even though this is not a complete explanation of what an annuity is, for me, the insurance the annuity provides is like the guardrails. The annuity can protect our investment with many guarantees. They keep us from disaster and tumbling over the side. For many of us, the major benefit of the guard rail is just getting us on the bridge in the first place.

I have found some clients will point to the increased expenses and decide against this potential solution and just end up buying CDs. They will argue the extra costs aren't worth it. I don't know about you, but I have never actually hit a guardrail. It is possible some of the guarantees of the annuity will never be used either. Perhaps this concern is shortsighted if the alternative meant you didn't participate with growth-oriented investments because of fear of falling off. As history tells us, over time, growth-oriented investments have well outpaced CDs, even with the fees associated with annuities. Have you ever hit the barrier?

> Cindy's husband, Clark, died leaving her his 401(k). She dedicated this money for their two sons. If at all possible, Cindy was never planning on touching this money, as she didn't need it and, hopefully, never would. Additionally, Cindy did not want to risk the principal in any way, so she was planning on rolling over CD after CD until she died. We discussed the principal guarantee annuities offer. This one offered a 100 percent guarantee her sons will at least receive the principal at her death. If the value of the account increases, then they would receive an even higher amount. There was no downside to this decision, so she moved this money into the annuity, selected a balanced portfolio (of coffee cups) and is tickled pink knowing the money can now grow with the market (less internal fees) and is guaranteed to their sons at her death. "I like my guardrails," she tells me.

Annuities can be very tricky investments. Make certain you work with a financial advisor that not only knows when you might need one, but also knows how to properly explain to you the pros and cons of annuities.

Tell Me More About the Taxes

The trick is to stop thinking about it as your money.

IRS Auditor

The best way to share with you the sometimes complicated taxes of annuities is to give you an example.

> Years before we met, a ninety-two-year-old widow bought a $50,000 non-qualified annuity with money from her savings account (that she had already paid taxes on). Over the years it grew to $250,000! Until this point, she paid no taxes on the $200,000 growth, allowing all of it to grow tax deferred. If she decides to cash out, she will pay ordinary income on the $200,000 growth. If she takes some out, she will pay taxes on all she takes out, until all of the gain has come out. Once she has pulled out all of the gain, she will have her original $50,000 left. This original deposit will come out tax free, because in the beginning she already paid taxes on that money. (In accounting terms, annuities are taxed Last In First Out (LIFO).)

One of the additional benefits of annuities is the internal grow is tax deferred. You pay no taxes on growth until the money is pulled out. The way annuities have worked for many years is the principal of your deposit is with after tax money, and any of the gain and growth grows tax deferred. Once you start withdrawing the money, you then have to pay the taxes on the gain first, as ordinary income tax. After you have taken out all of the growth (capital appreciation and dividends reinvested) you will get down to your principal. Because you have already paid the taxes on this (when you first made the deposit) you receive this money tax free.

Think of Thanksgiving dinner and homemade turkey gravy. After everyone enjoys the meal, there is gravy left over. You put it in the refrigerator. The next day you notice the gravy has settled to the bottom, and on the top is the fat. There are two layers: one gravy, one fat.

The gravy represents the money you put into the annuity, and the fat represents the increase or gain in value.

When you withdraw from the annuity, you are required to take out the fat first, then the gravy. So you are required to take out the increase in value first, then you can take out the principal.

If the annuity is purchased with qualified money (coming originally from an IRA, 401(k) or similar pre-tax investment), then all of it would be considered to be fat, because none of the money has yet to be taxed. It is all taxed when you pull it out, at your then income tax bracket. None of the money is after tax principal because in the year you invested it in, you received a tax break; therefore, when it comes out, it is all taxed at the ordinary tax bracket you are in at the time you withdraw the money.

Fixed Annuities

If the annuity is an umbrella with coffee cups protected by guardrails, then what is a fixed annuity? Quite simply, money deposited in fixed annuities is guaranteed by the company to earn the investor some fixed rate. Although not a CD, they can operate in very similar ways. The fixed rate quoted by the insurance company is for a certain number of guaranteed years. When the guaranteed period ends, the future rates are established typically like one-year CDs, that will just roll each year. (Fixed annuities are "loan" investments.) You typically have to keep your money invested for a period of years or there can be a surrender penalty.

Variable Annuities

Unlike the fixed annuity where the company gives you a promise to pay a minimum amount, the money deposited into a variable annuity goes into investments you select. These investments are similar to mutual funds, (technically called sub-accounts) as each option has a different goal and associated risk. You select which sub-accounts you want based on the risk you are willing to take. These investments act just like the coffee cups we learned about earlier. The amount of money you earn or lose is based upon the performance of the investments you picked.

As you think about annuities, keep in mind that they are simply umbrellas with coffee cups underneath them protected by guardrails. The coffee cups can be either fixed or variable. The guardrail guarantees will be different from fixed and variable annuities, so you will need to explore the one best for you. Like any investment, remember to check out the risks and fees, and read the prospectus carefully before investing.

> *As you think about annuities, keep in mind that they are simply umbrellas with coffee cups underneath them protected by guardrails.*

Advanced Topic: Annuitization and Immediate Annuities

There are two phases to an annuity (regardless of whether they are fixed or variable): (1) the accumulation phase and (2) the annuitized phase.

Until now, the discussion has centered on an annuity in the "accumulating" phase. It is growing within the umbrella, inside of coffee cups, surrounded by guardrails. You can change phases from accumulation to annuitization, but not the other way.

When you are in the accumulation phase, you do just that. You accumulate. You still have access to your money within certain penalties we talked about earlier. You maintain complete control over the account. You can:

- ∞ keep the money in this company, or after the contractual period is over, and there is no longer a surrender penalty, you can move it to another annuity.
- ∞ move an IRA annuity to another regular IRA or to another company.

ଔ have the company send you some of the contract value for your use.

ଔ start and stop income.

When you annuitize a contract, you lose complete control of the money. In essence, you turn over the accumulated money to the insurance company, and they in turn give you an income guarantee. You decide if the guarantee is for a period of time (like ten years) or if it is as long as you live (which could be more or less than ten years). When you annuitize, you select an income stream and the insurance company guarantees it.

Important tax rules need to consider before you annuitize. Make sure you speak with a financial advisor to discuss the "exclusion ratio," which is that part of the income that is taxable and that part which is a return of principal. The important lesson for us here is when you annuitize, you lose control of your money and your flexibility.

NOTE: Annuitization is not to be feared, it just needs to be understood. For example, think about when you selected (or when you will select) your Social Security payout. You have essentially annuitized your payout. Once decided, you no longer have any control; the option you selected is locked in forever and cannot be changed. Also, think about when you selected (or will select) your pension payout options from work (or if you are one of the lucky ones, your lottery payout options). Once selected, your payout option is locked in and you cannot make any changes. The annuity lock is the same when you annuitize, so be careful because that decision can generally not be undone.

Inherited Annuities

If you inherit an annuity, you need to pay special attention to the federal tax code and certain elections you will need to make within prescribed time frames based on the original owner's date of death. Just to make it fun (and complicated), qualified annuities have different federal timetables than non-qualified annuities. Inheriting an annuity can give you continued tax deferral and allow for the dividends to be reinvested and compounded, which is generally accepted to be the eighth wonder of the world. You will just need to be careful when dealing with annuities you inherit.

Thoughts

When you annuitize, you select an income stream and the insurance company guarantees it.

Annuities can be very complicated. Make certain you are dealing with someone who fully understands how they work, not just how to *sell* them.

Important Considerations:

Variable insurance products, including variable annuities are offered by prospectus only. The prospectus contains information about the product's features, risks, charges and expenses, and the investment objectives, risks and policies of the underlying portfolios, as well as other information about the underlying fund choices. Before investing, consider the investment objectives, risks, charges and expenses of the annuity and its investment options. Read the prospectus and consider this information carefully.

Principal value, income payments, and investment returns of a variable annuity will fluctuate, and you may have a gain or a loss when money is received.

Laws of a particular state or laws may be applicable to a particular situation may have an impact on the applicability, accuracy, or completeness of this information.

13

Trusts Made Easy

Do not be desirous of having things done quickly. Do not look at small advantages. Desire to have things done quickly prevents their being done thoroughly. Looking at small advantages prevents great affairs from being accomplished.

Confucius

A trust is a legal document established within current law to help you control your assets (ingredients) while alive and direct them upon your death. Significant legal considerations and contingencies exist when creating trusts and other documents, so it pays to seek legal advice concerning these types of documents.

I presume clients will always be confused about trusts, even those who have established them. As you would expect by now, I have an analogy to help you visualize how and why a trust works. Even if you never fully understand a trust, don't let them be an obstacle to achieving your goal. Trusts used correctly can be wonderful planning tools.

Trust

In your mind, take out a large keepsake box and open it up. Put it on the kitchen table. A trust is like that keepsake box. You can put items in the box, and you can take them out. You could put in a checkbook, a deed to property, car keys, and stock certificates. You can take them out.

Just like on the outside of a Campbell® Soup can you will see recipes and ingredients, the keepsake box has a set of instructions, recipes, and ingredients directing the transfer of the money. Whatever the grantor (the person who puts assets into the box) directs, then the transfer will flow accordingly.

While alive, the grantor can put in and take out whatever he or she wants to. But at the grantor's incapacity, due to death or illness, the box is then shut and locked closed. Only the assets inside the box are governed by the instructions on the outside. More than one box with completely different instructions on each may exist. That's why it's important to identify the different assets you have put into the trust. The recipe and ingredients on the outside will give instructions to the successor trustee as to how to handle the assets within.

The grantor can create an unlimited number of provisions and directions for the trust. Generally, the grantor directs under what circumstances the money is released and to whom. The trust therefore "flows" the money to those who will inherit it.

The law provides for many different types of trusts. There can be charitable trusts, special needs trusts, or revocable living trust, just to name a few.

Remember, the lawyer creates the trust; it is your job (and your financial advisor will help) to define your objectives and to move assets into the trust. Because you can have more than one trust, you will need to identify which trust is to control and distribute which asset. The way you move the assets into the trust is by titling them in the name of the trust you want them in. If they are not titled in the trust, they will not be governed by it.

Important Definitions

Grantor is the person who puts money into the trust. Normally you are the grantor, and you have the trust titled in your name. You are also normally the trustee of your trust.

Trustee is the person (or people) who has the authority over how the assets inside of the trust are managed within the guidelines of the trust itself. Normally with revocable living trusts, the grantor and the trustee are the same person.

Titling: Most trusts are titled like this:

The Shak Hill Trust
Shak Hill, Trustee
U/A 1/17/2017 (U/A stands for Under Agreement)

NOTE: You will see variations on how the account is titled. The name has no material meaning, but generally gives a clue as to what the purpose of the trust is. For example, the title might be The Shak Hill Revocable Living Trust, or The Hill Family Trust. If it was The Hill Children's Education Trust, then you would have a clue the money would be for the Hill children's education. (It does not have to give a clue. It could be called Trust No. 1.) Essentially, you choose the name within certain common standards. No one universal way dictates how *has* to be titled.

Successor trustee: The will has a personal representative or executrix; the trust has a successor trustee. This is the person or entity (like a bank trust department) who will succeed the original trustee when the original trustee either resigns or is unable to serve.

Co-trustees and co-successor trustees: The grantor can name co-trustees and co-successor trustees to serve. The grantor needs to be certain whether the intent is for them to work together or separately. This arrangement can be very burdensome, particularly if the "co" lives out of the area and they are required to work together. Then there is a need for both signatures on *every* transaction. This will mean overnight mail, lost mail, coordinating between work schedules, vacations, and illness. I have found that co-trustees sounds like a great idea, but in practical sense might not be. If you are concerned about one trustee taking advantage or having certain favoritism over another, then name an independent trust department where they will operate without prejudice.

Beneficiary: The person, people, or organization who will receive assets.

Purpose of Trusts

Now that we have talked about what trusts are and given some definitions, let's spend some time talking about their purpose. Through this discussion, you will begin to see if you need a trust based on your unique situation. Remember, not everybody needs a trust. Some women with modest means may absolutely need a trust, while some with significant assets might not need them at all.

Directs Your Money

The number one purpose of a trust is to "flow" your money. The trust lets you stagger money over time or give it out all at once. It lets you set thresholds of achievement, either naturally at certain ages or after certain accomplishments. You can put parameters on the distribution (flow) of the money to the beneficiaries based on whether certain deeds are done and whether certain deeds are not done.

Let me give you some examples, but know that the list of possibilities is unlimited.

- Once they are twenty-one, then they get "x" amount
- At age thirty they get "y" amount
- After they have graduated from college
- Once they are married
- After the birth of their first child
- When they have achieved their graduate degree
- If they are not in jail
- If they are not dependent on illegal substances
- As long as there is no criminal record
- If they join the military
- If they receive an honorable discharge

You have nearly complete control as to when, how, and under what conditions you flow the money. You can set benchmarks as described here based on accomplishments or transition the money merely based on age. You can restrict the flow if there is a history of irresponsible behavior or criminal activity. By delaying ownership of the assets when using the trust, you are allowing the recipient(s) time to mature and become more responsible as they accomplish certain tasks and achieve certain ages.

Additionally, if there are special-needs considerations, you can schedule an income

You have nearly complete control as to when, how, and under what conditions you flow the money.

stream and not let a special-needs child have access to the principal. You can start with an income stream, change to a lump sum, and return back to the income stream. Only your imagination limits to the possibilities when it comes to trusts.

As you can see, the choices are endless. You are in control with the use of a trust on how you flow the money and when. If you want to restrict the flow of money, you cannot do that with great detail under a will, so a trust is best.

> Barbara's net worth is $1,350,000 when you include her home. She has two sons. One is responsible. He is married and has Barbara's only three grandchildren. The other son has never been married and has been in jail for minor offenses twice. Barbara wants the first son to have his portion of the inheritance at once without restriction on her death. She wants the second son to "clean up" his act; then he can get his money after he gets his college degree, holds a white-collar job for over a year, and stays clean for five years. At each of these three events, she has directed the trustee to release him some of the money.

Barbara needs a trust because she wants to flow the money under certain circumstances to her second son. She can name the responsible son to be the successor trustee, or her bank, or anyone else that she chooses. A will alone does not work.

Takes Advantage of the Applicable Exclusion and Tax Planning

The second reason for a trust is to take advantage of your applicable exclusion that is allowable under federal law. This is the amount that you can shelter upon your death, free from federal estate tax, to your heirs. The part of your estate above this amount will have a tax consequence.

Federal law has continually changed the amount of the exclusion and keeping up with this continual change can be daunting. The firm Cannon Financial has dedicated resources to make understanding these changes fairly easy. You may want to review their Tax Guide at www. cannonfinancial.com/uploads/main/2015FederalTaxGuide.pdf. If you have a large estate – over $5 Million, you will want to review this guide. Make sure you have an estate planning attorney on your professional management team to ensure you take advantage to important inheritance tax avoidance laws.

Avoids Probate

The third important benefit of the trust is to avoid probate. Probate is the legal means a state uses to transition your assets from you to your beneficiaries.

As you know, every citizen is a citizen of a state. For me, I'm a Virginian. As such, Virginia (as well as all states) has a legally defined last resort or fall back position in which to process or transition my assets to my heirs. This legal process is called probate. Probate can be costly and will delay the transfer of my assets to those who will eventually end up with them.

By using a trust, you outline a legally recognizable document with your wishes of how the money is to flow. Because you have taken this step, trust assets bypass the probate process and go directly to the trust for the named beneficiaries as outlined in the trust. Because probate is generally the last resort, if you do almost any planning, your plan could prevent your estate from having to deal with probate.

Helps Win Estate Challenges

The fourth benefit comes if your estate is challenged. The instructions and wishes of a trust are often viewed to be harder to challenge than those of a will. For example, if a will was created very near death, then there could be a challenge as to whether it was properly executed, whether the writer was of sound mind, or if there was undue pressure or coercion of any kind. In contrast, if the trust had been in place over the last six months, or six years, and has been operating normally, the trust can be deemed to be a truer representation of the wishes of the deceased.

Don't be fooled here. I have spoken with many attorneys who repeatedly tell me they make a good living based on the lawsuits arising from trusts. Just because you have a trust doesn't mean there won't be a challenge. It just means the courts won't have to probate the asset, which has *absolutely nothing* to do with whether there is a challenge or not.

Protects Privacy

The fifth reason for a trust is privacy. The will is a public document for all to see. The trust is not. Many say this is a good thing; after all, why is it other people's business how your assets are going to transition? On the other hand, because there is little oversight, no one is watching the successor trustee to ensure the wishes are being carried out as desired. Unfortunately, the successor trustee may not always act in the best interest of the deceased, but in his own best interest. There are always pros and cons to everything.

Privacy can also be a detriment if the grantor of the trust becomes incapacitated and the successor trustee has a vested interest in the remaining assets at the grantor's death.

Let me give you an example of this. Let's say you have created a trust and you have named one of your two daughters to be the successor trustee. You become ill and unable to handle the trust. Your daughter now becomes the successor trustee making financial decisions for this money and for your care.

If she is the beneficiary as well, there will be a conflict of interest. Does she spend top dollar for your care and risk depleting funds she would otherwise receive at your death? Your daughter might think, "Mom is going to die soon anyway; she doesn't even recognize me." I have witnessed firsthand when quality care was restricted so more money will be left for the beneficiary. This is a sad and unfortunate possibility. Because the other daughter is a beneficiary, she will have the ability to know what is going on, but the court and other family or general public will not.

The will is a public document for all to see. The trust is not.

Other Considerations

Many clients think that just because they have a trust means they won't be paying any taxes. Not true. Remember, income tax is never forgiven, so even if your estate is below the estate tax threshold, money that is income - such as retirement plans and the gains in annuities - will *always* incur income tax. Also, those who have wealth in excess of the applicable exclusion threshold will still have to pay applicable death taxes. Consider Bill Gates. Just because he has created trusts (which I can only presume), he doesn't skip paying taxes. The trusts will flow the money, which is the number one reason for trusts in the first place, but they won't avoid the tax after the exclusion amount is used.

Trusts can also be used in advanced estate planning. There are a number of trusts available, designed to shelter assets from current tax law. Trusts can generate income for you while you are alive with the remaining principal going to charity. Other trusts transition your residence to your heirs while alive in a very tax-efficient manner. Still others will help transition assets if your spouse is not a U.S. citizen. Still other trusts are used for special-needs children. Please consult a well-qualified attorney to discuss these important strategies.

We have discussed trusts and the functions they provide. Trusts have wonderful benefits, but be aware, like anything else, you may get *sold* a trust even if you don't necessarily need one. Not all lawyers who sell trusts will tell you you don't need one. Many people out there have bought a trust they really don't need. Just make certain you need one before you pay for one.

Funding the Trust

Just because you have taken the time and the expense to set up a trust doesn't mean you're finished. You need to "fund" those assets into the trust you want governed by the trust. Like I said earlier in the book, the best analogy I use is simple to explain.

The attorney builds the house; it is your job to move in the furniture.

Remember, to do this, you have to re-title all of the assets you want in the trust. The checking account, savings, brokerage, money market, and car, as well as beneficiary changes to 401(k), IRA, and annuity contracts all need to be re-titled into the trust (if you want them to be governed by the trust).

Check with your attorney as to the wisdom of titling your personal residence into the trust. Some states, such as Florida, give strong protection to homeowners and, generally, it might not be in your favor to title your home in the trust. Florida gives protection to individuals, not trusts. In Virginia where I live, the protection is not strong.

Thoughts

Each state has their own rules and laws governing trusts. Please use this information as educational and not specific to any state. It is important to contact a competent estate planning attorney to coordinate your situation to the laws of the state you live in.

———

The attorney builds the house; it is your job to move in the furniture.

———

14

Long-Term Care Insurance

When you get to the end of your rope, tie a knot and hang on.
Franklin D. Roosevelt

Almost every one of my women clients is concerned about long-term care insurance (LTC). LTC is becoming more popular as the need is becoming more real. The odds of needing this type of care are greater than your house burning down or getting into a major car accident.

As a married couple, a husband and wife make a solemn pledge to care for each other in good times and in bad, in sickness and in health. If he is no longer able to care for you or if something happens to you, who is going to take care of you? Sometimes we can turn to our kids, but they should be raising their families and living their lives.

Many women will turn to LTC to help fill in the gap.

The Basics of LTC Insurance

Benefits are generally computed in the following way.

> The number of days that you want
> covered X (multiplied by) the benefit
> paid for those days.

Let's say you want to cover three years in care and you project to need $200 per day.

365 days X 3 years X $200 = $219,000 of benefit available.

You will pay a premium based on your age and health when you purchase the policy. If you need care and the actual cost per day is below your projected daily benefit, then the amount of money you pull out will be less than what was projected. If a portion of your daily benefit remains unused, you do not lose this unused money; it remains in the pot for future use, allowing you to stretch more days of coverage.

On the other hand, if the cost of care is greater than the daily benefit, you are only able to pull out the contractual daily benefit. You will have to find another source to make up the difference.

Six Daily Functions

LTC policies will generally start paying benefits if you can only perform four out of six daily living functions. Without thinking about it, we all perform the six daily functions routinely and automatically. However, as we move forward in our life cycle (as we age), these tasks may become challenging. The six daily functions are:

• **Feeding** – taking the food from a plate and getting it into your mouth without help.
NOTE: Someone else can prepare the food.

• **Transferring** – the ability to move in and out of bed or chair without assistance.
NOTE: The use of a mechanical aide is acceptable.

• **Continence** – having complete control over urination and bowel movements.

• **Bathing** – the ability to bathe oneself or need help with only a single part of the body, such as the back or a disabled limb.

• **Dressing** – the ability to get clothes from the drawer and put them on, including fastening shirts, buttons and buckles.
NOTE: They may need help with tying shoes.

• **Toileting** – going to the toilet and getting on and off the seat. Keeping genital areas clean without help.

Physically, we might be able to perform these functions, but mentally we might not remember to do them. This condition will generally qualify for benefits.

Mentally, we remember to perform these functions, but physically we might not be able to accomplish them. This condition will generally qualify for benefits.

Qualifying for a Policy

When you apply for a LTC policy, the insurance company will do a medical evaluation. They are looking for your *morbidity* risk, not your mortality risk. In general terms, morbidity risk is the likelihood you will get sick, and mortality risk is the likelihood you will die. Life insurance looks at mortality; LTC looks at morbidity. Even if you haven't been able to get a life insurance policy, you may very well be eligible for a LTC policy.

> *Even if you haven't been able to get a life insurance policy, you may very well be able to get a LTC policy.*

Added Considerations

There are many additional benefits you need to consider when purchasing a policy.

• Is the daily benefit inflation protected?
• Do you have longevity in your family? How long should you have coverage for? Some policies will pay benefits for life.
• Does the policy only cover you if you are in a facility or will it cover you if you want care to be at your home?
• Which carrier to go with?

Thoughts

Research the quality of the company you buy the policy from. Many independent companies rate insurance companies. I would absolutely go with at least an A rated company or better. Make certain you not only look at the rating as of today, but get a track record. Many quality companies are AAA rated. After recent credit quality issues, you should go with a strong company even if they have a slightly higher premium. Obviously, it will do you no good if you make a claim to a company that has failed.

15

Common Mistakes You Must Avoid

An economist is an expert who will know tomorrow why the things he predicted yesterday didn't happen today.
Laurence J. Peter

Throughout this book, real-life incidents help bring home important points. There is also a need to discuss some points in greater detail to help you recognize that real problems exist and common mistakes are made. My goal is to enable you to prevent such mistakes.

Check Beneficiaries

Fred was divorced and just married Jill. Fred had rewritten his estate planning documents, pointing all assets to Jill. He even went out of his way to disclaim his ex-wife. Jill quickly found she was pregnant, and both she and Fred were excited about starting their family. Fred was killed instantly when a drunk driver ran a red light as Fred was coming home from work.

As Jill reviewed his assets, she unfortunately discovered that Fred did not change the beneficiary on his personal life insurance policy as well as on the company life insurance policy. Both of these payouts went to the ex-wife.

Remember, contracts like life insurance are not governed by the will. Jill was the beneficiary on the 401(k), but this had not grown nearly enough to make an impact on Jill and their unborn child.

The importance of how an account is titled is often overlooked. This is one of the most common mistakes made. Earlier we talked about Joan and her three daughters and how she had titled her money in the local daughter's name. Here is another reason why you have to review how assets are titled.

Carmen married Bill who was divorced with two adult children. They were married for sixteen years when at age 70, Bill died unexpectedly. In settling the estate, Carmen discovered the title of their home was in the name of Bill and his ex-wife. Well the good news for Carmen was the ex-wife died before Bill. The bad news is because Bill died without a will, his estate was governed by intestate laws. In his state, the law gives two-thirds of his assets to children and one-third to his wife. Bill has two sons who now each own a third of the house Carmen is living in. I immediately had Carmen go to the attorney and draft a "life estate" for the two sons to sign. They both did, but they didn't have to. Carmen could have been forced to sell and relocate from the home she wants to live in for the rest of her life.

I have probably purchased fifty hot tips in my career,
maybe even more.
When I put them all together, I know I am a net loser.

Charles Schwab

Not Creating Estate Documents

Anna was married to Steve for 52 years when he died. They had three children (and six grandchildren). After a couple of years, Anna began attending a singles group sponsored by her church. At age 75, she met and married Chuck. Two years later, Anna died.

Even though she had pre-purchased her funeral arrangements years ago (before Steve died), Chuck made all of the decisions.

When the children argued their mom and dad had even purchased side-by-side burial plots and that he was to be buried there, Chuck would hear nothing of it. He had Anna buried at his family plot.

Although less than the applicable exclusion credit amount, the estate of Mike and Ginger topped $5 million. Because it was lower than the exclusion, they didn't bother creating estate documents. When Mike was diagnosed with Alzheimer's, he was declared incompetent and Ginger was named his court-appointed guardian. She had to travel down confusing estate planning considerations, medical decisions, business dealings and other issues concerning with Mike she was unfamiliar with, at the worst time in her life. Bank accounts in his single name were frozen. Business accounts were inaccessible. End of Life decisions were not expressed in the Living Will. Burdened with all of this, Ginger had a nervous breakdown.

Both of these situations, and hundreds more that I have personally dealt with, could have easily been eliminated with proper estate planning documents.

NOTE: All kinds of issues surround minor children when no estate planning document exists. Who will be their guardian? Who will manage any inherited money? Where will they live, and who will raise them? Of course, other important matters like education and medical treatment greatly impact children. The will provides for the parents to name whom they designate as those responsible for the children if something happens to both of them. Without a will, in my opinion the first and most critical estate planning document *all* must have, then a judge will decide. And even if the judge gets is right, the process will be contentious and expensive.

Government Savings Bonds

While they are guaranteed by the government for interest owed and repayment of principal at maturity, they don't create wealth. This next point is important. After taxes and inflation are considered and you take into account the money could have been invested in other areas, there is an argument you are just barely breaking even, if not losing.

Many people just buy these bonds and forget about them, often times sticking them in a safe box. In fact, according to the www.treasurydirect. gov web site, there are savings bonds no longer earning interest of any kind still out there held by unaware investors.

The Bureau of Public Debt estimates there are 33 million matured bonds worth more than $13.5 billion.* That is to say, they are no longer earning any interest. Zero. Zip. Nada.

If you have a U.S. Savings Bond Series, know this:

- A, B, C, D, E, F, G, H, J, K bonds are no longer earning interest.
- EE, I, and Saving Notes only earn interest for thirty years.
- HH earn interest for only twenty years.

You may want to go onto www.treasurydirect.gov to see if your bonds have matured. Check your safety deposit box for any of these bonds.

* http://www.treasurydirect.gov/news/pressroom/pressroom_comtreasuryhunt.htm

Additionally, at death, bond have no step-up in cost basis. The interest is taxable to the current owner no matter how long (or short) that person owned the bond. Interest is treated as ordinary income at the tax bracket of the owner at the time of the redemption.

As you create your long-term plan, tell your advisor about any government bonds you have and see how, if at all, they fit with your new plan.

Protect Yourself, Get It in Writing

If you have any type of verbal agreement anywhere, get that agreement transferred to paper. As formal as it may be with best friends or family, events are now different, and you need to protect yourself.

> Marie lives with Frank. They are not married but have been together for twenty-five years. He has two children from a previous marriage, and she has none. She is sixty-seven, and Frank is approaching seventy-four. He is on dialysis and awaiting a kidney transplant. They keep their finances separate.

> When I met them, I discovered the house is owned by Frank and his will leaves everything to his two children. I spoke with Frank and Marie at length about where Marie was going to live when Frank dies. He insists the children, who after all these years have accepted their relationship, will allow her to live in the house when he dies. I strongly encouraged Marie to get a legal "life estate" to live in the house or some kind of legal document allowing her to live there after he dies, even if he lives another ten to fifteen years. I am saddened to report that, as of this printing, she has done nothing to protect herself.

It Is Okay to Sell Your Husband's (Parent's) Stock

A certain emotional connection exists when it comes to a husband's property and his investment accounts (even if they were in joint name). After his death, you may feel a connection to him vicariously through this property or these stocks and mutual funds. Many psychologists agree that keeping these assets near gives a sense of his presence and that, by selling them, there is somehow a violation of his wishes or a breaking of the connection. This feeling can be very strong - yet concerning.

There can be a belief that "if I hold on to this, then I am still holding on to him," or "if I let go of this, I am letting go of him."

The life goals the two of you had included these possessions as part of the overall plan. But now it is just you, these possessions may need to be transitioned to best meet your individual goals.

As harsh or cold-hearted as this may sound, the wishes of the dead are not as important as the reality of the living and, at best, their wishes are based on old information. He would expect you to make needed changes for your best interests now that he is gone.

Here are a couple of stories I would like to share with you to help you see this emotional connection is real, this bonding is felt by many, and it is normal to feel it.

> *As harsh or cold-hearted as this may sound, the wishes of the dead are not as important as the reality of the living and, at best, their wishes are based on old information.*

Story #1: In 1999, I was working with a widow whose husband had worked over forty years for the pharmaceutical company Pfizer. This company is well known for their drug Viagra. He was a simple man who worked as a "sanitation engineer" and did cleaning maintenance work at their plant. She told me that forty years earlier, Pfizer granted him one share of stock for a job well done. This happened again; thirty-nine years ago, another stock. You see what was happening: thirty eight years ago, another at thirty-seven, and so on for each year he worked there. He was granted stock as he continued to work. In the course of Pfizer's growth, he reinvested the dividends and stock splits occurred along the way.

When I met her through church, she was eating peanut butter and jelly and struggling to make ends meet. At seventy-one, it was definitely not supposed to be this way.

She shared with me that in her husband's desk drawer (and not even in a safety deposit box) were those stock certificates he had earned over the years. A relatively huge stack! "Oh, those are his," she said shyly, "and I could never sell them. I don't even know what they are worth."

After spending many hours speaking with her, we agreed he was collecting these stocks so "one day" they would be sold and used to supplement retirement. I then gave her permission to sell them because "one day" was now. We sold the stock at near the all-time high of $150 per share. The proceeds were turned into income-generating bonds (she did not need growth, she needed income) generating nearly $2,000 of income per month. Needless to say, she stopped eating peanut butter and jelly.

Story #2: Mike was a day-trader. During his spare time, he spent much of it reading, learning, and watching his stock account. He traded daily and sometimes even traded intraday. He knowingly built this portfolio on risky "plays" in the market and the latest hot-stock tips. He unfortunately got ill and, within a very short three months, passed away.

I met his daughter Martha six months after the funeral. She showed me his portfolio and this particular account. I knew she had not picked them and the associated risk with these stocks was great. "I can't sell them," she said almost in tears. "He studied the market daily and he picked these. I trusted him his whole life, and I am not going to let him down now that he's gone."

I took my time and asked her about his trading pattern. We both agreed he was in and out of the market constantly. I was thankful when she realized because of his pattern of trading, he would have definitely sold those particular stocks by now. We did just that and started creating a long-term plan that provided increasing income for the rest of her life.

Be Aware of Certain Types of Investments

Anything promising quick returns with little or no risk, avoid like the plague. Unfortunately some will pressure you to buy something, even tell you it is guaranteed, and you will get rich quick. No such thing. Not now, not ever.

Never buy any type of hot tips or "ground floor" opportunities or exclusive offerings only available for a short amount of time. The salesperson will try to give you the impression you have to act before the opportunity is over. This "time pressure" has trapped many, don't let it trap you.

Be very wary of the salesperson who tries to become your new best friend. I heard of a life insurance salesman who went after widowed women. He was well-dressed and articulate. He took his prospects out to lunch, sent them cards, and even called them "Mom" if they let him. He became the "son" they never had. Only after he wore them down did they buy from him, if for no other reason than "he was so nice to me."

After the sale, he was gone.

Don't buy anything with guaranteed profits or interest rates that sound too good to be true. Even if they hand you something saying insured, or worse - FDIC insured - it could be a scam in the making. Of course, after the sale, the salesman is nowhere to be found.

Ask the Bank

As hard as this piece of advice is, but true, be aware of the family member with seemingly good intentions. Many times a son-in-law or brother-in-law knows you now have money he can use. He will tell you what he believes is the best opportunity to make even more money. Perhaps he will buy a business or start one. Perhaps he knows a friend who is making big money, and he wants you to be a part of it. Resist with all of your might. Hopefully your daughter will not join in, but your gut reaction will be the best.

You might want to call your financial advisor, banker, accountant, attorney, or friend and run the idea by them and have your son-in-law call them as well. If after his discussion they think it is a good idea for you, then they will let him know. If not, they will tell him as well.

Either way, you have used someone else as a sounding board. You get to blame them when they say no. You could say, "Well [substitute family name here], I sure did think your idea had merit. I am not sure why my financial advisor said no, but he knows finances better than I do, and this must not be part of my comprehensive plan. I am sorry he said no, but I am going to stick with his decision." This way you get to blame them for the decision, even though you knew it wasn't a good one in the first place.

This way you get to blame them for the decision, even though you knew it wasn't a good one in the first place.

You may also want to go to the loan officer at your local bank. Bring your son-in-law with you. Share the idea with a professional who approves loans as a living. Make sure the banker pulls his credit report. If the loan officer wouldn't do it (and you know he wouldn't), then blame it on the banker!

Diversification

I met Suzanne a couple of years ago. She and her husband were from Atlanta and were solid middle class. Together they had purchased the stocks of several local banks and reinvested the dividends. Over the course of many years, one bank was bought by another. Their stock grew in value, but the number of holdings got smaller with each buyout. Eventually, each and every bank they owned was merged and became the same bank. She now had all of her stock, over $1.3 million, in one company.

With her pension and other income, she lives off the dividends coming from this concentrated holding. I have recommended many times she diversify, spread out her risk, but to no avail. I even asked her a backwards question, "If you came to me with $1.3 million in cash, what would you think of my recommendation if I suggested we put every last penny into one bank stock? How would you feel?"

I do believe banks are strong, but with recent financial issues, I'm not so sure. Either way, she is grossly over concentrated. This bank stock represents 80 percent of all of her holdings. If the stock market corrects, a mutual fund will correct with it, but over time mutual funds should return value if the underlying holdings are solid. The problem with one (or few) stock(s) is they might go to zero! With the diversification of a mutual fund, eighty to a hundred stocks in one fund, even if one goes to zero, the rest can come to the rescue and keep you from losing everything. My rule of thumb, you should never have over 5% of your portfolio in any one stock. You will most likely have more than 5% in your mutual fund, which is okay as your mutual fund in turn has many holdings inside of it.

Another Diversification Story

When I was continuing my education years ago, I remember seeing a stock certificate of the International Mercantile Marine Company. This was the company that built the *Titanic*. Yes, the company went bankrupt when the *Titanic* sank. On the stock certificate was an endorsement from the registrar, Bankers Trust Company, authenticating the certificate. The transfer agent was JPMorgan. The stock was purchased for $550,000.

Instead of the investor putting all of the money into one company, if he had diversified a third into the International Mercantile Marine Company, a third into Bankers Trust Company, and a third into JPMorgan, it would be worth well over $60 million today. Even with a third of the money going bankrupt with International Mercantile Marine, Bankers Trust Company is now Bank of America and JPMorgan is now JPMorgan Chase Company. In this case he would have been much better off diversifying, but remember, diversification itself cannot eliminate the risk of investment loss.

16

Move Forward and Create Your Own Recipe

It's not the plan that is important, it's the planning.
Dr. Graeme Edwards

Now it's your turn. We have discussed important aspects of financial planning and who is best suited to help you accomplish your goals and dreams.

I have given you **A RECIPE** to help with your planning but the best recipe is the one you create. Review the seven essential ingredients we discussed. Make certain you start with emergency cash and then allocate money for known extras.

When this is done, now you have the luxury to take more risk, and you *should* take more risk. Not wild dot.com risk, but prudent, well-thought-out, spread-your-eggs-across-many-baskets plan to minimize the risk and maximize the return. Add in some cash, CDs, stocks, bonds, mutual funds, and annuities to taste. You want to have a personal coffee cup flavor you enjoy. Mint chocolattè tastes much better than dirt. Put your investment ingredients in risk order based on your goals and time available to reach those goals. Create your own Wayshak Pyramid®. Use professionals to help you with your plan.

The first step is to consider your legacy and the message you want to leave to your loved ones. Write down in your own words what your goals are. Write down what is important to you. Is it vacationing and traveling? If so, write down how many trips you want to go on and where you would like to go. Is it starting a new career or opening up your own business? Is it taking care of the children or grandchildren?

Next, think about your expenses. Write down in general terms how much you spend every month and what amount of emergency cash you need to feel comfortable. Also, make note of any upcoming extras you expect within the next four years or so. Is there a new car, boat, vacation home, or wedding coming up? Do you need a new roof on the house, how about a deck, or other home improvements? Whatever your extras are, write them down.

Now, consider your income. Identify the money coming in, where it is coming from, and how much you receive monthly.

Make note of any life insurance, disability insurance and long-term care you have, or you want.

Last, jot down all of your assets and liabilities. Put down bank account holdings (not the account numbers), CDs you have, savings accounts, and checking. Put down if you have stocks, bonds, or mutual funds. List any 401(k), IRA, and brokerage accounts. Even put your U.S. Government Savings Bonds that might be hidden away in your safety deposit box. Add any other assets like annuities, life insurance, property, and business ownerships.

Put down all of the debts you have: car payment, credit cards, mortgage, and other debts and the interest rate you are paying for each. Put everything down.

Now you're ready.

Ask for some references from your friends as to who they use for financial planning. Search for the estate planning council in your area. Go onto the CFP web site, www.cfp.net and look for a CERTIFIED FINANCIAL PLANNER™ professional in your area. You can also look at the Financial Planning Association (FPA) for their listing of professionals. Their web site is www.fpanet.org. This professional organization is dedicated to the advancement of financial planning and the ethical conduct of their members.

Interview several investment advisors to see if there is a fit. There has to be some kind of chemistry between you and the person you are interviewing. Don't be in a hurry to hire someone; enough advisors are out there so you should have a pretty good selection. Bring the information you wrote down, share this during your interview, and let the planner come up with a recommendation.

Look for the individual who takes his or her time to learn about *you* and not just your *money*. Make sure he or she is looking to solve your concerns and not meet their sales goal. See if they care about your life's story and not just about selling a product. If they are not looking for a long-term relationship with you, then don't hire them.

CAUTION: In my opinion, many investors take the warning "don't put all your eggs in one basket" to mean you have to hire several advisors and give each of them some of your money so you have "spread it out." If you use an accountant, you don't take the first six months of receipts to one accountant and the second six months to another. How would you ever get a coordinated tax return? What you do is hire one accountant for all your receipts, donations, expenses, charitable gifts, etc and that one accountant manages all this for you.

> *Look for the individual who takes his or her time to learn about* you *and not just your* money.

To carry this one further step, I bet you only have one dentist. You don't give one dentist just the top teeth and another one your bottom. Take your time and hire one financial coach who has the expertise to handle all of your baskets. They should not put all your eggs in one basket, but should spread you among several. They will be able to manage all of them for you.

Thoughts

We never know how long we have to live. This is one of the great unknowns in life. One thing is certain, you will either live long or live short. You shouldn't plan on living short, and your finances shouldn't be only in short-term investments. My clients plan on living long, and their financial plan is consistent with their lifelong goal. Some folks say, "I don't even buy green bananas anymore." But the clients I like best are telling me of the flower garden they just planted and ask me if I would like some of the seeds for myself. Create a long-term plan for yourself. Create **A RECIPE** for your life and only use the best ingredients!

My goal for you is that you plan a long life and, while alive, you live.

*Create **A RECIPE** for
your life and only use the
best ingredients!*

*My goal for you is that
you plan a long life and,
while alive, you live.*

Charts and Tables

Historical Annual U.S. Inflation Rate from 2000 through 2016

YEAR	JAN	FEB	MAR	APR	MAY	JUN	JUL	AUG	SEP	OCT	NOV	DEC	AVG
2016	1.37	1.02	0.85	1.13	1.02	1.01	0.84	1.06	1.46	1.64	1.69	2.07	1.26
2015	-0.09	-0.03	-0.07	-0.20	-0.04	0.12	0.17	0.20	-0.04	0.17	0.50	0.73	0.12
2014	1.56	1.13	1.51	1.96	2.13	2.07	1.99	1.70	1.66	1.86	1.32	0.76	1.62
2013	1.59	1.96	1.47	1.06	1.36	1.75	1.96	1.52	1.18	0.96	1.24	1.50	1.47
2012	2.93	2.87	2.65	2.30	1.70	1.66	1.41	1.69	1.99	2.16	1.76	1.74	2.07
2011	1.63	2.11	2.68	3.16	3.57	3.56	3.63	3.77	3.87	3.53	3.39	2.96	3.16
2010	2.63	2.14	2.31	2.24	2.02	1.05	1.24	1.15	1.14	1.17	1.14	1.50	1.64
2009	0.03	0.24	-0.38	-0.74	-1.28	-1.43	-2.10	-1.48	-1.29	-0.18	1.84	2.72	-0.34
2008	4.28	4.03	3.98	3.94	4.18	5.02	5.60	5.37	4.94	3.66	1.07	0.09	3.85
2007	2.08	2.42	2.78	2.57	2.69	2.69	2.36	1.97	2.76	3.54	4.31	4.08	2.85
2006	3.99	3.60	3.36	3.55	4.17	4.23	4.15	3.82	2.07	1.31	1.97	2.54	3.24
2005	2.97	3.01	3.15	3.51	2.80	2.53	3.17	3.64	4.69	4.35	3.46	3.42	3.39
2004	1.93	1.69	1.74	2.29	3.05	3.27	2.99	2.65	2.54	3.19	3.52	3.26	2.68
2003	2.60	2.98	3.02	2.22	2.06	2.11	2.11	2.16	2.23	2.04	1.77	1.88	2.27
2002	1.14	1.14	1.48	1.64	1.18	1.07	1.46	1.80	1.51	2.03	2.20	2.38	1.59
2001	3.73	3.53	2.92	3.27	3.62	3.25	2.72	2.72	2.65	2.13	1.90	1.55	2.83
2000	2.74	3.22	3.76	3.07	3.19	3.73	3.66	3.41	3.45	3.45	3.45	3.39	3.38

(notice the deflation in 2009 and 2015)

http://inflationdata.com/inflation/Inflation_Rate/CurrentInflation.asp

Average 20 year Nominal Return from 1995-2014

9.9%	6.2%	1.1%	2.4%
Stocks[1]	Bonds[2]	Cash[3]	Inflation[3]

In order to calculate the <u>real rate of return</u> and your purchasing power, you have to take into consideration inflation. Your purchasing power would look like the following after the effects of and inflation:

Average Real Return of Return after inflation:

7.5%	3.8%	-1.3%
Stocks	Bonds	Cash

If you had your money in CDs and savings accounts, you lost purchasing power!

[1]S&P 500 Index
[2]Barclay Total Bond Index
[3]J.P. Morgan Asset Management

Actuarial Chart

Age	Male life expectancy in years	Female life expectancy in years	Age	Male life expectancy in years	Female life expectancy in years
20	57.07	61.63	61	20.67	23.52
21	56.13	60.66	62	19.90	22.68
22	55.20	59.68	63	19.15	21.85
23	54.27	58.71	64	18.40	21.03
24	53.35	57.74	65	17.66	20.22
25	52.42	56.76	66	16.93	19.42
26	51.49	55.79	67	16.21	18.63
27	50.56	54.82	68	15.51	17.85
28	49.63	53.85	69	14.81	17.09
29	48.69	52.88	70	14.13	16.33
30	47.76	51.92	71	13.47	15.59
31	46.83	50.95	72	12.81	14.86
32	45.90	49.99	73	12.18	14.14
33	44.96	49.02	74	11.55	13.44
34	44.03	48.06	75	10.94	12.76
35	43.10	47.10	76	10.34	12.09
36	42.17	46.15	77	9.76	11.44
37	41.24	45.19	78	9.20	10.80
38	40.31	44.23	79	8.66	10.18
39	39.39	43.28	80	8.13	9.58
40	38.46	42.33	81	7.62	9.00
41	37.54	41.39	82	7.14	8.43
42	36.62	40.45	83	6.68	7.89
43	35.71	39.51	84	6.23	7.37
44	34.81	38.57	85	5.81	6.87
45	33.91	37.65	86	5.40	6.40
46	33.02	36.72	87	5.02	5.94
47	32.13	35.81	88	4.65	5.52
48	31.26	34.89	89	4.31	5.12
49	30.39	33.99	90	4.00	4.75
50	29.53	33.09	91	3.70	4.40
51	28.68	32.19	92	3.44	4.08
52	27.84	31.30	93	3.19	3.79
53	27.01	30.42	94	2.97	3.53
54	26.19	29.54	95	2.78	3.29
55	25.38	28.67	96	2.61	3.08
56	24.57	27.80	97	2.46	2.89
57	23.78	26.93	98	2.33	2.72
58	22.99	26.07	99	2.21	2.56
59	22.21	25.22	100	2.09	2.41
60	21.44	24.37			

https://www.socialsecurity.gov/OACT/STATS/table4c6.html

Here are the results if you invested in the DOW Industrial Average on the worst day of the year (market high) or the best day (market low).

Investing on the *worst day* to invest
(the highest market day of that year)

Market High	Cumulative Investment	Value at End of Year
12/13/1995	$10,000	$9,418
12/27/1996	$20,000	$20,517
8/6/1997	$30,000	$36,324
11/23/1998	$40,000	$54,500
12/31/1999	$50,000	$73,073
1/14/2000	$60,000	$85,767
5/21/2001	$70,000	$90,633
3/19/2002	$80,000	$85,492
12/31/2003	$90,000	$117,629
12/28/2004	$100,000	$138,776
3/4/2005	$110,000	$158,415
12/27/2006	$120,000	$193,278
10/9/2007	$130,000	$213,864
5/2/2008	$140,000	$146,122
12/30/2009	$150,000	$195,399
12/29/2010	$160,000	$226,255
4/29/2011	$170,000	$231,199
10/5/2012	$180,000	$276,946
12/31/2013	$190,000	$376,499
12/26/2014	$200,000	**$431,612**

Average annual total return 7.3%

Investing on the *best day* to invest
(the lowest market day of that year)

Market High	Cumulative Investment	Value at End of Year
1/30/1995	$10,000	$12,182
1/10/1996	$20,000	$26,038
4/11/1997	$30,000	$46,023
8/31/1998	$40,000	$68,588
1/22/1999	$50,000	$91,017
3/7/2000	$60,000	$104,865
9/21/2001	$70,000	$111,061
10/9/2002	$80,000	$105,936
3/11/2003	$90,000	$147,083
10/25/2004	$100,000	$172,005
4/20/2005	$110,000	$194,581
1/20/2006	$120,000	$236,603
3/5/2007	$130,000	$261,117
11/20/2008	$140,000	$181,776
3/9/2009	$150,000	$246,718
7/2/2010	$160,000	$285,374
10/3/2011	$170,000	$291,414
6/4/2012	$180,000	$347,927
1/8/2013	$190,000	$473,393
2/3/2014	$200,000	**$542,140**

Average annual total return 9.0%

Here is the CD rate of return.

Year	Total	Rate of Return	Value at the End of Year
1995	10,000	5.98%	$10,598
1996	20,000	5.47%	$21,724
1997	30,000	5.73%	$33,542
1998	40,000	5.44%	$45,911
1999	50,000	5.46%	$58,964
2000	60,000	6.59%	$73,508
2001	70,000	3.66%	$86,565
2002	80,000	1.81%	$98,312
2003	90,000	1.17%	$109,580
2004	100,000	1.74%	$121,660
2005	110,000	3.73%	$136,571
2006	120,000	5.24%	$154,252
2007	130,000	5.23%	$172,842
2008	140,000	3.14%	$188,583
2009	150,000	0.87%	$200,311
2010	160,000	0.44%	$211,236
2011	170,000	0.42%	$222,166
2012	180,000	0.44%	$233,187
2013	190,000	0.27%	$243,844
2014	200,000	0.27%	**$254,529**

Average annual total return 3.16%

http://www.federalreserve.gov/releases/h15/data.htm

Glossary

401(k), 403(b), 457 plans: employer-sponsored retirement plans offered to eligible employees. Employees contribute their money and the company can match.

Annuities: an investment option that is offered through insurance companies. There are two kinds, either fixed or variable. Fixed annuities have a guaranteed payout, and variable annuities are invested in accounts that have market exposure. While in annuities, money grows tax-deferred, which can be very beneficial. Annuities can be turned into guaranteed lifetime income streams.

Asset allocation: spreading your investments across different asset classes, such as stocks, bonds, CDs, mutual funds. Through asset allocation, you generally will lower your overall risk.

Assets: all of the things that you own.

Beneficiary: the person or persons whom you choose that will receive part of your assets when you die. On contractual investments (like life insurance, retirement accounts, and annuities) and in trust documents, you name a beneficiary.

Bond: an investment in the debt of corporations or government entities, like the state, county, city, or federal. The issuing authority guarantees the timely payment of interest owed and the return of principal at maturity.

Bond fund: a mutual fund (or coffee cup) that is invested in bonds. Bond funds are invested in corporations and have taxable interest. Muni-bond funds are invested in government debt and usually have tax-free interest.

Brokerage firm: a company that is licensed to sell investments to the general public. These companies are governed by many agencies, including FINRA.

CD: a certificate of deposit. CDs have a variety of maturity times and generally the longer you are willing to lend your money to the issuer, the higher the interest they should be willing to pay you.

CERTIFIED FINANCIAL PLANNER™: a professional designation offered by the Certified Financial Planning Board of Standards. A person holding the CFP® must pass comprehensive educational classes in Financial Planning, Insurance Planning and Risk Management, Employee Benefits Planning, Estate Planning, Investment Planning, Income Tax, and Retirement Planning. The CFP® practitioner must also agree to a high degree of ethical standards.

Chartered Financial Consultant (ChFC®): As the financial world became more complicated, the ChFC was created in 1982 to further enhance the insurance professional. As important as the CLU is, the ChFC takes the next step by including financial planning and wealth creation. The American College (www.theamericancollege.edu) confers this professional designation. The ChFC professional also has strict continuing educational requirements that have to be met as well as professional standards of conduct combined with ethical training.

Chartered Life Underwriter (CLU®): designation established in 1927. The CLU professional is highly educated with a rigorous educational program, has required experience in the field, and can provide a wide range of financial planning and insurance expertise. The American College (www.theamericancollege.edu) confers this professional designation. Continuing education is required to maintain the CLU designation as well as professional standards of conduct combined with ethical training.

Defined benefit plan: a company retirement plan that will pay an eligible retiree a defined, predetermined benefit. Sometimes the retiree has the right to take a lump sum amount or can elect monthly payments.

Defined contribution plan: retirement plans employers offer to their employees, such as 401(k), 403(b) and Th rift Savings Plans (TSP). Employees have the right to define their contribution amount, typically added each pay period, and determine their investments within those available through the plan. Employers may choose to match contributions as an additional employee benefit. The employee has to reach a certain age to withdraw accumulated funds without federal penalty and has to begin annual withdraws at age seventy-and-a-half.

Diversification: the attempt to decrease investment risk by selecting a wide range of investments, including stocks, bonds, mutual funds, annuities, and life insurance. By spreading out your investments, you are seeking to lower risk and not put all your eggs in one basket.

Durable Power of Attorney: a legally recognized document that allows an individual to grant permission to another to have the right to make decisions on their behalf. Once given, this power continues until revoked and can be used by your designee with or without your consent.

Estate Planning Documents: those legally executed documents that define your estate plan. There are four documents in most estate plans: a will, a durable power of attorney, a health care directive, and a trust.

Financial Advisor: a person you hire to help you manage your financial plan. Almost anyone can call themselves a financial advisor. There is little industry oversight as to the determination of what makes a person a financial advisor. The consumer should exercise caution as to the experience, expertise, knowledge, and credentials when hiring a financial advisor.

FINRA: Financial Industry Regulatory Authority is the largest independent regulator for all securities firms doing business in the United States. www.finra.org.

Health Care Directive: the legal document that establishes the person or people that will make health related decisions for you when you are unable to make those decisions.

Inflation: the overall increase in the price of goods and services. This increase is measured by the government and can be easily checked at www.inflationdata.com. Historically, inflation has been relatively low (below 4 percent).

IRA (Individual Retirement Account): unique definition from this book: a coffee cup filled with ingredients covered by an umbrella. A retirement account that grows tax-deferred until you withdraw from it. It is taxed at your ordinary income tax rate when pulled out.

Joint Tenants with Rights of Survivorship (JTWRS): legal title that is held by more than one person. All parties have rights to the money, and at the death of one of the owners, the remaining owner(s) receives the money. By "operation of law" this asset is immediately available to the joint owner regardless of the value. JTWRS assets are not governed by the will or the trust.

Law of Large numbers: the belief that in a pool composed of many people, some will live short, some will live normal lives and some will live long.

Non-qualified money: money already exposed to income tax.

Probate: the legal process that transitions your assets governed by the will from you to your beneficiaries. The legal document that names the guardians of your minor children.

Qualified money: money not yet exposed to income tax. If this money has never been taxed, like 401(k), 403b, IRA and similar retirement deposits, then this money is considered to be 'qualified' money.

Roth IRA: an individual retirement account that is funded with aftertax dollars. The investment grows tax deferred and is withdrawn tax free.

Stock: ownership in a company. The owner shares in company growth, dividends, and has a right to vote on the direction of the company. The owner also has the risk of company losses.

Stock Fund: a mutual fund (or coffee cup) that is invested in companies. Stock funds are invested in corporations and have the potential to outpace inflation overtime. They can have increased risk and volatility.

Titling: the important legal way an asset is owned. Do not underestimate the need to check on how you own your assets. After reading this book you may need to adjust how your accounts are titled.

Trust: the legal document created to flow money at incapacitation and death. Many forms of trusts exist creating wonderful control and tax advantages.

Will: the legal document that directs the transfer of your estate assets after your passing. The will is also used to name a legal guardian for your minor children or disabled adult child. Assets governed by the will go through the probate process.

Bibliography

Armstrong, Alexandra, and Mary Donahue. <u>On Your Own</u>. Chicago: Dearborn, 2000.

Barney, Colleen, Esq., and Victoria Collins, PhD, CFP®. <u>Best Intentions, Ensuring Your Estate Plan Delivers Both Wealth and Wisdom</u>. Chicago: Dearborn Trade Publishing, 2002.

Bove, Alexander, Jr. <u>The Complete Book of Wills, Estates & Trusts</u>, 3rd ed. New York: Owl Book, Henry Holt and Company, 2005.

Chatzky, Jean. <u>Make Money Not Excuses</u>. New York: Random House, Inc., 2006.

Clifford, Denis. <u>Estate Planning Basics</u>, 3rd ed. Berkeley, CA: Nolo, 2005.

Lenhart, Gloria. <u>Planet Widow: A Mother's Story of Navigating a Suddenly Unrecognizable World</u>. Emeryville, CA: Seal Press, 2006.

Perry, Ann. <u>The Wi$e Inheritor</u>. New York: Broadway Books, 2003.

Stovall, Jim. <u>The Ultimate Gift</u>. Colorado Springs, CO: RiverOak, 2001.

INDEX

About the Author

Shak Hill is a CERTIFIED FINANCIAL PLANNER™ professional, a Chartered Life Consultant, a Chartered Financial Consultant and holds a Masters Degree in Finance. His financial practice has gravitated towards the woman clients. He adds significant value by taking time to explain the sometimes complicated financial world and making it easy to understand. He loves to teach and help enhance the overall level of understanding of financial planning and the importance of creating your unique financial recipe.

Another area of great concern to Shak is to help those who have been diagnosed with serious medical conditions, like cancer or a need for organ transplants. During this incredibly stressful and frightening time, Shak can help consolidate financial matters, simplify the financial web of accounts, statements and such, as well as ensure that you have proper estate planning documentation in place. Shak's wife Robin is a very healthy bone cancer survivor, after an initial diagnoses of six months to live. Shak is an organ donor and on the national bone marrow transplant list. He donates blood every 56 days, without fail. He has been there; he has walked in your shoes; let him help you and your family.

Also written by Shak to support others with a life threatening diagnosis is *When the Doctor Says It's Cancer: A Caring Financial Plan For Life.* This work focuses on the important need to continue financial planning when there is a diagnosis or end of life issue. Once you hear cancer or transplant list or other life threatening disease, your family's focus shifts to treatment, prognosis, diagnosis and how to defeat the disease, but important financial considerations must be attended to. This work will be invaluable if you know of someone who is now living with difficult medical considerations.

A gifted speaker, Shak is available for presentations to your group about updated and timely financial topics. He can also be a key note speaker about working with the widow and the importance of understanding the challenges she faces, and also the importance of financial planning when the doctor has said there is cancer or life threatening diagnosis. If you are interested in working with Shak regarding your personal finances, feel free to contact his office in Northern Virginia at publisher@ GuidingLightBooks.com. Shak is a father of six children and has been a foster father of forty six. He and Robin live in Centreville, VA.

You can order more books on line at your favorite book web site, or through GuidingLightBooks.com. For bulk discounts, please feel free to contact the publisher.

Make It a Great Day To Live!

Your Financial Guiding Light™

www.GuidingLightBooks.com
Publisher@GuidingLightBooks.com

This material is not intended to provide legal, tax or investment advice, or to avoid penalties that may be imposed under U.S. Federal tax laws, nor is it intended as a complete discussion of the tax and legal issues surrounding retirement investing. Contact your tax advisor to learn more about the rules that may affect individual situations. The author does not provide legal or tax advice. For legal or tax advice, please seek the services of a qualified professional.

17 26

CPSIA information can be obtained
at www.ICGtesting.com
Printed in the USA
LVOW11s1723020317
525947LV00003B/525/P